THE
IMAGINATION'S
NEW
_BEGINNING

Theology and Modern Literature

UNIVERSITY OF NOTRE DAME
WARD-PHILLIPS LECTURES IN
ENGLISH LANGUAGE AND LITERATURE

Volume 1

Frederick J. Hoffman

THE
IMAGINATION'S
NEW
BEGINNING

Theology and Modern Literature

Notre Dame & London

UNIVERSITY OF NOTRE DAME PRESS

PN
49
H62

FOREWORD

THE FOUR LECTURES WHICH MAKE UP THIS BOOK
were given at the University of Notre Dame in the
first week of May, 1966, by Frederick J. Hoffman,
Distinguished Professor of English at the University of Wisconsin-Milwaukee. They were the first
of an annual series newly established under the
auspices of the Department of English, the Ward-
Phillips Lectures in English Language and Literature.

The series is named in honor of two deceased
members of the English faculty, Reverend Leo L.
Ward, C.S.C., and Professor Charles Phillips, both
of whom were writers as well as teachers. Father
Ward's stories of farm life in his native southern
Indiana appeared in such distinguished "little mag-
azines" as the *Midland* and have since been collected in the posthumously published volume, *Men
in the Field*. Professor Phillips published several
books, including collections of poems and critical
essays, plays, and a biography of Paderewski.

However, these two men are remembered chiefly
for what they did as teachers to advance the study
of letters among their students and colleagues. After a brief career of only nine years at Notre Dame,
Professor Phillips, at the time of his death in 1933,

had earned a place as one of the great teachers in the history of the University. He had also taken an important part in establishing the University Theater. Father Ward began teaching English at Notre Dame in 1929, and as head of the department from 1936 until his death in 1953, he did much to give our department its distinctive, creative character.

We take pride, then, in presenting this publication by our University Press, and we are especially grateful to Professor Hoffman for inaugurating our Ward-Phillips Lectures with a work of such originality and distinction as *The Imagination's New Beginning*.

Ernest Sandeen, *Head*
Department of English
University of Notre Dame

PREFACE

READERS WHO KNOW MY BOOK, *The Mortal No: Death and the Modern Imagination* (Princeton University Press, 1964) should find easy ways of associating the present series of lectures with it. In fact, I regard this book as the third of a series that have much to do with each other: the first was *Samuel Beckett: The Language of Self* (Southern Illinois University Press, 1962). All three are concerned with a common set of literary and moral phenomena in twentieth-century culture. Like the great poet he is, Wallace Stevens offers an abundance of suggestions which can be elaborated upon and "filled in," by discourses that are characteristic of discourses in criticism, philosophy, and theology.

The title of this book shares with *The Mortal No,* among other things, its source in Part VIII of Stevens' poem, *Esthétique du Mal.* The special relationship contained within these lines gains strength when one looks at the poet's words.* Stevens projects (momentarily, as it proves) a world in which there are no "phantoms"—that is, formal patterns and designs which recreate the world without de-

---

* The lines appear on page xiii, immediately preceding the beginning of the text.

priving us of a sense of its essential meanings. When these are gone, the "shaken realist" has to see "reality" (what he elsewhere calls "things as they are") unadorned and unrelieved. In these circumstances, "the mortal no"—death without assurance of a continuation of any kind into eternity—has a powerfully depressing effect on men of the imagination, who characteristically depend on some assurance of immortality. But, in a turn of dialectic that a reader of Stevens comes to expect, the very loss of the "phantoms" puts pressure upon the poets to reconstitute the forms which superintend reality and allow us to see and understand it.

At this point the phrase I have chosen for the title of my book occurs, "the imagination's new beginning." And the phrase is significant for Stevens' poem, as it is accurately descriptive of the content of my lectures. The writers I discuss here (they are limited in number, and should be considered in association with those of the other two books I have mentioned) are essentially engaged with the kinds of reflection that are best defined by the title phrase. They have themselves, individually, taken over a part or much of a religious system, or a set of religious emotions, and have tried to look at them in the light of a temporary or a permanent disillusion, then have engaged in two kinds of dramatic speculation: either to describe what happens without the symbols of religious systems, or to recreate these symbols in terms of a teeming world, alive with both variants of "the mortal no" and the stresses

and strains of "the yes of the realist spoken because
he must/Say yes. . . ."

I first attempt a general statement of the points
at issue; I have used Yeats and Stevens to help illustrate my argument in the first chapter. Inevitably,
Joyce plays a significant role in these discussions.
Chapter two of the present work should be seen as
a supplement to my treatment of Joyce in *The Mortal No.* The essay here is more explicitly limited
than the earlier study, but it gains strength and conviction from having been treated in depth. Explicitly, in this chapter I examine the relationship
between Joyce as actual creator and Stephen Dedalus as his most challenging and demanding creature. The growth of this relationship is of the essence
to a study of Joyce's struggle with both the theology
and the provincial culture of his native Dublin. The
subject is all but inexhaustible; I do not claim that
I have exhausted it here, but I have tried to define
it and to discuss it at reasonable and useful length.

Chapters three and four are concerned with one
of the most absorbing practices in modern literature and culture, the dramatization of Christ's death
in terms of the various patterns of meaning and
emotional consequence that death has. I have chosen as various a set of representations as I can,
though I have not done so simply for the sake of
virtuosity. Each of the three examples is vitally and
powerfully meaningful in its own context and for
its own sake. At the beginning of chapter four, I
have turned to a subject not unrelated to the major

one I have already described: the relationship of man's interest in the religious monuments of the past to his sense of a lack in taste and culture in his present circumstance. The two themes come together in the vast and complex metaphor of Chartres Cathedral, as that is seen by Henry Adams.

The occasion of these lectures was a very special one. I was asked by Ernest Sandeen, chairman of Notre Dame's English department, to inaugurate the annual Ward-Phillips Lectures, which I presented on the afternoons of May 2, 3, 5, and 6. I am deeply indebted to Professor Sandeen, not only for the invitation, but for many kindnesses which helped to make my stay on the Notre Dame campus so pleasant. There are many other people who assisted at one time or another—at luncheons or dinners or in informal gatherings—in impressing upon me the friendliness and the genuine charm of Notre Dame. I am also grateful to the Director of the University of Notre Dame Press, Emily M. Schlossberger, and to Grant Lee for their services in helping me to set up the lectures for publication.

Frederick J. Hoffman

CONTENTS

	Page
Foreword	v
Preface	vii
Definitions and Responsibilities	1
The Hardness of Reality: Joyce's Stephen Dedalus	21
The Friends of God: Dostoevsky and Kazantzakis	49
Nostalgia and Christian Interpretation: Henry Adams and Faulkner	75
Index	103

xi

> . . . How cold the vacancy
> When the phantoms are gone and the shaken realist
> First sees reality. The mortal no
> Has its emptiness and tragic expirations.
> The tragedy, however, may have begun,
> Again, in the imagination's new beginning,
> In the yes of the realist spoken because he must
> Say yes, spoken because under every no
> Lay a passion for yes that had never been broken.

WALLACE STEVENS,
Esthétique du Mal

DEFINITIONS AND
RESPONSIBILITIES

1

NO ONE WHO HAS BEEN CURIOUS ABOUT RECENT speculations on the relation of theology and literature can have failed to notice the appearance of a number of studies affecting it.[1] I think the several books have at least these matters in common: first, the assumption that literature (as distinguished from sociologies, political sciences, and philosophies) has a special *rapport* with the distinct nature of a world in crisis; second, an acceptance of the fact that neither religious thought nor romanticism in its critical or literary expressions is altogether useful or precise in defining the current intellectual gestalt; third, a special skill (very different, for example, from the skills of the "new critics") in allowing literature to yield a particular kind of evidence in support of philosophic disquisition.

We have long been aware of the varieties of religious crisis in the nineteenth century; in many respects this is as much a nineteenth- as it is a twentieth-century problem. In the early decades of our century, the discussions of literature and religion were largely supported by the assumption that although there were crises, traditional Christianity had "held firm." Earlier critics rarely if ever suggested that Christianity was threatened; they were mainly satisfied to note deviations from its pure center.

One must emphasize the roles that logic and rationality play in this literature over a period of several centuries. I should like here to suggest a feasible summary of the developments leading to our present sense of crisis. We began with Cartesian speculations, which depended fundamentally upon a power of mathematical descriptions of certitudes and a willingness to forego skepticism concerning God's role in the management of the universal machine. From this point, rationality took over; that is, a reasonable world was assumed, and much of literature attended to manners and conventions, with a range of useful ironies that acted as a check upon human absurdities. The essential terms of self-definition shift, however, from the basis of *je pense* to that of *je me doute*. It is hard to establish a date for the beginnings of doubt, but there is no question that the focus changes from a level of assumed manners to one of uncertain selves. At first these uncertainties are only relative to the strength of original confidence from which they have declined. But gradually and steadily the fact of inquiry merges with the character of the inquirer.[2]

Another way of putting it is that metaphysics gave way to the strategies of epistemology and to the creation and the maintenance of secular and formal worlds. Samuel Beckett, who was writing an essay in explanation of Joyce's *Finnegans Wake,* set the tone of literary criticism in 1929 when he described Joyce's work as "purgatorial," and went on to describe that term as meaning the "absolute absence of the Absolute. Hell is the static lifelessness of unrelieved viciousness. Paradise the static lifelessness of unrelieved immaculation. Purgatory a flood of movement and vitality released by the conjunction of these elements."[3] This is as unorthodox a conception of the three terms as we are likely to get. Nevertheless, according to it we may say that Beckett's work is itself largely "purgatorial": the self in his writings is continually "relating" to its world, and conducting what appears to be an all but ceaseless analysis of this relation. There is a tension set up by the conflict between our normal desire for transcendence (in the present, but mainly in the ultimate, post-mortem future) and reality itself, seen without any formal or metaphoric disguises.

The fact is that, without the power of transcendence with which theologians have been endowing gods, and critics poetry, reality remains suspended between Hell and Heaven, in the "absolute absence of the Absolute." In his book *Poets of Reality* (1965), Professor J. Hillis Miller says that "A new kind of poetry has appeared in our day, a poetry which grows out of romanticism, but goes beyond it. Many twentieth-century poets begin with an experience of the nihilism which is one of the possible consequences of romanticism."[4] The romantic nature begins by assuming both an objective and a subjective reality, and by answering eschatological questions in terms of a reality beyond itself; but gradually faith in the objective reality is shut off, and an extreme form of ego-sensitivity sets in. In some ways this difficulty comes as a consequence

3

of the assumption that the self *creates* reality, which is in fact no longer objective.[5] This is a turn from the earlier assumption that a Being who exists beyond our powers of creation is in fact responsible for our existence.

2

THE MAJOR CRISIS FOR THE MODERN ARTIST IS THAT of a ceaseless wrestling with reality, with the not altogether clearly defined aims of recreating God in the artist's image, finding surrogate forms for those he has chosen or been forced to deny, and creating a substantive world that—although dependent upon him since he is the creator of it—nevertheless satisfies as an object of belief. The clash of ideology and theology in our century, which has had serious consequences for both, has affected adversely the metaphoric distinction between the grounds of each.[6] Some of the original revolutionaries in Russia must have thought ideology a more than adequate substitute for religion, since it was an act of putting eternity within time and locking its forms, so that they could become available to administrative and managerial controls. That these hopes were illusory is testified to again and again in our literature,[7] but the disturbing facts of our world include the suspicion that *all* kinds of formal containment are false or at least inadequate.

There is much speculative improvisation about

how the mind may "make it on its own" by either assuming a set of moral limits or forming a creature greater than itself. Perhaps the most important speculation of all involves having eternity and the real usefully and significantly converge. Some variant of the Incarnation symbol is to be found in the work of almost every important writer; and in writers whom we continue to respect—or at least do not abandon reading—the search for a means of establishing a form of Incarnation takes on quite personal qualities, usually because it is a conclusion derived from the experience of spiritual struggle. Like most cultures, ours has had one of its major crises in the problem of facing mortality and speculating about what if anything lies beyond its occasion.

Of course there is always a percentage of speculation concerning either the possibility or the fact of a total "absence of the Absolute." Joyce's Leopold Bloom, his modern "Ulysses," puts the matter this way, as he observes the funeral ritual for Paddy Dignam, who like his Homeric ancestor, Elpenor, has died as a consequence of overdrinking:

> . . . Seat of the affections. Broken heart. A pump after all, pumping thousands of gallons of blood every day. One fine day it gets bunged up and there you are. Lots of them lying around here: lungs, hearts, livers. Old rusty pumps: damn the thing else. The resurrection and the life. Once you are dead you are dead. That last day idea. Knocking them all up out of their graves. Come forth, Lazarus! And he came fifth and lost the job. Get up! Last

day! Then every fellow mousing around for his liver and
his lights and the rest of his traps. . . .[8]

Bloom here appears to be the hardest type of "no-
nonsense" realist. Actually, as we all know, Joyce
finally makes of him something of a romantic, and he
possesses more than the usual sentimental fear of
nihilism. In more recent literature there is some attempt to "hide" from a reality by the device of making the real world absurd, and therefore intolerable.
In consequence the literature seems cynical and
sometimes actually is so. This little poem of Günter
Grass may illustrate the trend, though many of the
French *nouveaux romanciers* are also implicated:

> In our museum—we always go there on Sundays—
> they have opened a new department.
> Our aborted children, pale, serious embryos,
> sit there in plain glass jars
> and worry about their parents' future.[9]

I am inclined to think that most writers are concerned about the problem of "framing" mortality in
some religious or humanistic way—as we may see in
this short poem by Lisel Mueller, called "On Finding a Bird's Bones in the Woods":

> Even Einstein, gazing
> at the slender ribs of the world,
> examining and praising
> the cool and tranquil core
> under the boil and burning
> of faith and metaphor—
> even he, unlearning

6

> the bag and baggage of notion,
> must have kept some shred
> in which to clothe that shape,
> as we, who cannot escape
> imagination, swaddle
> this tiny world of bone
> in all that we have known
> of sound and motion.[10]

The major issue is still that of universalizing experiences; the alternative course seems to reduce itself
to the practice of suffering the particulars in space to
move in some form of restrictive time scheme. That
this matter is not exclusively a twentieth-century
concern is testified to in the results of Hillis Miller's
analyses in the study of nineteenth-century English
poetry, *The Disappearance of God*. Professor Miller
speaks in his introduction of "the gradual withdrawal of God from the world."[11] The word "withdrawal" is more accurate than "disappearance,"
since he wishes really to suggest God's inaccessibility
to the human imagination. Modern literature does
describe the gradual removal of God from man. One
of the key metaphors is that of the abyss, used in
the nineteenth century by Baudelaire to indicate
both the almost hopelessly immense space between
man and God and the great anguish suffered between one instant of time and another.[12] Speaking
of De Quincey, Miller describes a "sense that at
every moment each man hangs over a moral abyss,
a feeling that he can never foresee all the results of
any act, an experience of anticipatory guilt, since

any act is bound to be in some degree evil, and an exaggerated sense of scrupulous responsibility." (*Disappearance,* p. 60) In a letter to a friend Flaubert expressed much of the same sense of loss and anxiety:

> One says to oneself, "Ten years ago I was there," and one is there and one thinks the same things and the whole interval is forgotten. *Then it appears to you, that interval,* like an immense precipice in which nothingness whirls round.[13]

3

The crucial point for the modern imagination is the suggested or real point of the Incarnation. Eliot expressed it this way in "Dry Salvages," the third of *Four Quartets*:

For most of us, there is only the unattended
Moment, the moment in and out of time,
The distraction fit, lost in a shaft of lightning
Or the waterfall, or music heard so deeply
That it is not heard at all, but you are the music
While the music lasts. There are only hints and guesses,
Hints followed by guesses; and the rest
Is prayer, observance, discipline, thought and action,
The hint half guessed, the gift half understood, is Incarnation.[14]

Whether or not this is a simple assertion of the real, it emphasizes a central issue in modern literature. This issue may be expressed in several ways: How can the eternal be made real? what is permanent (or eternal) about "things in themselves"? We can restate the question in this way: can "things" be reconstituted into new formations of reality, or do they just "bubble" and "effervesce" in their finitude? Can the universal (God, eternity, the Logos) be made to "touch down" upon the "bubbling" world of particulars, or do we simply imagine transcendence to begin with? We may say that the universals remain constant throughout and that literatures differ only in their ways of apprehending and defining them. Twentieth-century literature has been produced in a time of redefinitions, in which the burden of proof concerning reality appears to rest with the individual artist. Changes in style, in "experimental" writing, are themselves a sign of struggle, the poet searching in a whirl of particulars for standards of universal form, for the stillness about which the world moves.

Two general characteristics in modern writing seem to come from this condition: the extraordinary mixtures of doubt and assertion in it (in Unamuno, for example, in Malraux, in E. A. Robinson, in Yeats, and in Wallace Stevens); and the tendency, noticeable especially in modern American literature, to exalt the "thing" above the universal. As Tony Tanner of Cambridge University has said of this latter condition, perhaps it emerges from a not too clearly apprehended notion of Emerson that the "thing" was a portent of the transcendent real; in other words, the unproved confidence that "any object, not matter how trivial, was a 'symbol' of God and could serve as a 'window' to 'infinitude'."[15]

Two principal metaphors seem to engage all serious writers who concern themselves with both of these matters: the first, the Incarnation, is a major desideratum (that is, for the most part the "man of imagination" seeks a transcending means and a universal source); the second involves the validity of things, sensed as the result of an effort to present their precise "dinglichkeit" as vividly as possible. How these two come together makes for interesting speculation. There is what Hillis Miller calls the "new immediacy," in which the comprehensible particular survives the loss of a transcending power. (*Poets of Reality,* pp. 10–11) The tendency is strong in our time to separate metaphor from doctrine, or to give metaphor an arcanic power. It does not argue a lack of faith so much as a loss of tried and true ways of manifesting it. Theological necessities are as strong as ever; the desire for transcendence remains. Literature is as important a resource for the metaphoric elaboration of the theological view as it ever was, and the variety of ways in which metaphysical questions are first framed and then answered is a part of the brilliant kaleidoscope that is modern literature.

4

Perhaps the evidence is best drawn from modern poetry. Since I do have the privilege of selecting my evidence, as well as the responsibility of defending it, I should like to choose Yeats and Stevens as the major representative poets. Both of them struggled to define essences independently of current and past theological uses. Both seemed to think it necessary to come to terms with reality within poetry itself. And both finished with schemes of interpretations that were in many respects unique. They were not priests or doctors of the church; they were poets. In this sense they were "heresiarchs" in the manner of most men of letters who choose to follow their imagination's dictates. But if anyone were to chart the boundaries of both theological and metaphysical truths, they would assuredly be working within them.

If indeed one can describe him at all accurately, Yeats began by rejecting both Christianity *and* modern science. But *rejection* in this case does not mean what is might ordinarily signify. He was persistently concerned to define, in himself and for himself, all of the theological terms which he had apparently abandoned. At the center of his concerns was his own view of the imagination, which is as sensual as it is spiritual. Speaking about the poem "Leda and the Swan," Hillis Miller describes the "problems" of Yeats as well as any critic has in my experience:

> . . . He has come to see the universe as a great dance or sexual embrace. Energy flows outward from God until the physical world is made almost divine, and then flows back toward God, only to ebb once more toward the world. The relation between the earthly and divine realms is that of interpenetration and withdrawal, the momen-

11

tary ecstasy of revelation, the irrational cry, Leda's submission to the swan, followed by the creation of a culture
which slowly decays as "confusion falls upon our
thought," until a new revelation comes at last. . . .

(*Poets of Reality,* p. 118)

Not only here,[16] but in many other poems, Yeats
demonstrated his earnest wish to comprehend both
the universal and the particular, without losing the
strength and significance of either. He had a powerful sense of the meaning of transcendent being; he
was also aware of the strength of the human passions
and wished to preserve them in his imaginative con-
ceptions. Beyond these qualities, his writings show
a strange but emphatic sense of history, as though he
were personally to attend upon its events and to
direct their influence upon present and future. This
sense of history is linked importantly to his distrust
of modern science, which he desperately hoped to
replace by whatever stratagem at his command.
There is the truly terrifying play upon the second
coming, a symbol of the deterioration of the human
personality as he saw it:

> Surely some revelation is at hand;
> Surely the Second Coming is at hand.
> The Second Coming! Hardly are these words out
> When a vast image out of *Spiritus Mundi*
> Troubles my sight: somewhere in sands of the desert
> A shape with lion body and the head of a man,
> A gaze blank and pitiless as the sun,
> Is moving its slow thighs, while all about it
> Reel shadows of the indignant desert birds.

Definitions and Responsibilities

> The darkness drops again; but now I know
> That twenty centuries of stony sleep
> Were vexed to nightmare by a rocking cradle,
> And what rough beast, its hour come round at last,
> Slouches toward Bethlehem to be born?
>
> (*Poems*, p. 402)

The dreadful image is of course the antithesis of what Yeats desires. His greatest vision is of the union of the divine and the human, though even in this association the results are as happy as the act is intelligently and consciously committed. He is quite aware, for example, that the image of Leda and the swan may very well have been corrupted by indifference on the part of Zeus and unawareness on Leda's part; hence the act may very well have resulted, as he says, in "The broken wall, the burning roof and tower/And Agamemnon dead." (*Poems*, p. 441) Whatever their ultimate purpose, the poems are almost invariably fixed to boundaries of particular sensations and history—for practical reasons. Although the effects are not entirely satisfactory at the beginning, when Yeats tried to make Irish tradition and myth provide the limits, even here they served to keep his imagination from going out of bounds.

Yeats did not wish to destroy faith, but he honestly thought belief to be difficult if not impossible in our age.[17] For this reason he tried to contain "beliefs" within the symbolic and dramatic structures of his work, with the argument that the only way in which poetry can be philosophical is by portraying

13

"the emotions of a soul dwelling in the presence of certain ideas."[18] In any case, nothing that was purely spiritual could be accepted; whatever idea or symbol was in question, it had to run the test of a submission to human passion. In the end this insistence led to the celebration of imperfect man, whose intensity and passion gave both strength and dignity to experience. They were in a sense Yeats' version of the Incarnation, the point at which eternity intersected time. Despite his practice of shying away from Christianity, Yeats was fascinated by the metaphysical suggestiveness of Christ. The Incarnation remained a central attraction for him, though he preferred his own definitions of it. He was not "God-intoxicated"; as Ellmann says of him, he had "only to think of God to become sober and extremely wary." (*Identity*, p. 55) This was because he feared the "withdrawal" of God, the danger that He would become an abstraction and thus destroy the particulars of human existence.

As Yeats surely knew himself, it was difficult to maintain a balance between abstractness and particularity. Achievements of the communion of time and eternity were rare, though they became more frequent in the verse following 1920. He tried too many artificial contrivances in the earlier verse; and the complications of the prose work *A Vision* (1925) did not always lead to the best verse. Nevertheless, if Yeats seldom offered us the "moment" of apprehension of the infinite, there were some occasions when he made us aware of the move between

14

the mystic vision and the "pragmatical pig." Wallace
Stevens has left a heritage of poems that thrive exactly upon that motion. He is perhaps our greatest
poet, after Yeats, at least partly because he is capable of what Ezra Pound has called "super-positions."

Stevens calls our attention to elaborate and what
seem to be ceaseless variants upon unlimited themes;
there are thirteen ways of looking at a blackbird,[19]
but a thousand other ways as well, of looking at
reality.[20] Despite his intellectual complexity, Stevens
will not give in easily to the temptation to make a
spiritual out of a physical thing. He will go so far as
to suggest a transcendent reality, as he does in the
poem "A Primitive Like an Orb"; but this reality is
made of "major poems" nourishing each other and
endowed by some reality above them:

> We do not prove the existence of the poem.
> It is something seen and known in lesser poems.
> It is the huge, high harmony that sounds
> A little and a little suddenly.

The "central poem," which may suggest to us the
ultimate "concrete universal," is after all made from
human desires and joys:

> Their words are chosen out of their desire,
> The joy of language, when it is themselves.
> With these they celebrate the central poem,
> The fulfillment of fulfillments, in opulent
> Last terms, the largest, bulging still with more.[21]

I think I can conclude in some confidence that

15

the thrust toward universals is surely a strong characteristic of modern literature. It is not the only way of testifying to the significance of human experience, but it is perhaps the most fully tried, the most elaborately documented, and (at least in Western civilization) the most satisfactory resolution of particular doubts and misgivings. The primary difference from other times is that the exercise is a personal one. The imagination rules and is active, and there is little inclination to accept preordained metaphors. The religious imagination is stronger perhaps than it has been in most literatures, because of the need to establish new formulations of the central theological metaphors. Responsibility and need have both led to redefinitions. Poetry has been enlivened as a consequence; it has not remained static, but is in a constant process of being revitalized.

NOTES

1. Some of the more significant books which present the problems of this change are these: Maurice Friedman, *Problematic Rebel: An Image of Modern Man* (New York, Random House, 1963); Karl Adam, *The Christ of Faith: The Christology of the Church* (New York, Pantheon Books, 1957); Gabriel Vahanian, *The Death of God: The Culture of Our Post-Christian Era* (New York, Braziller, 1961); Vahanian, *Wait Without Idols* (New York, Braziller, 1964); John Killinger, *The Failure of Theology in Modern Literature* (New York, Abingdon Press, 1963); Charles I. Glicksberg, *Literature and Religion* (Dallas, Southern Methodist University Press, 1960); Julian N. Hartt, *The*

Definitions and Responsibilities

Lost Image of Man (Baton Rouge, Louisiana State University Press, 1963); and Gerhard Szczesny, *The Future of Unbelief,* trans. E. B. Garside (New York, Braziller, 1961).

2. With some revisions, this summary is taken from my book, *Samuel Beckett: The Language of Self* (Carbondale, Southern Illinois University Press, 1962), p. 79. See also this passage, on p. 60: "From his being a 'thinking thing,' whose *cogito* confidently anticipates his *sum,* the self has become a groping, stammering, hesitant, fearful thing, a *res haesitans.*"

3. In *An Exagmination Round His Factification for Incamination of Work in Progress* (New York, New Directions, 1962), p. 22; originally published in London by Faber and Faber, 1929.

4. *Poets of Reality* (Cambridge, Massachusetts, Harvard University Press, 1965), p. 1. Other references to this book will be found in the text.

5. Perhaps the best studies of this peculiarity of modern thought are Miller's *Poets of Reality,* mentioned above, and Erich Heller's *The Artist's Journey into the Interior and Other Essays* (New York, Random House, 1966). See my review essay, "Critics and Reality," in *Kenyon Review,* 28 (March, 1966), 282–88.

6. See Henri de Lubac, *The Drama of Atheist Humanism,* trans. Edith M. Riley (Cleveland and New York, World Publishing Co., 1963); originally published in this country by Sheed and Ward in 1950. For twentieth-century aspects of the problem, see my book, *The Mortal No* (Princeton University Press, 1964), ch. 2, pp. 94–135.

7. See Stevens' "Owl's Clover," a poem originally published in 1937, but omitted from the *Collected Poems;* it *was* republished in *Opus Posthumous* (New York, Alfred Knopf, 1957), pp. 43–71. Here Stevens distinguished between "the man that thinks" and the "man below," who "Imagines and it is true. . . . "(p. 66) The decision not to publish in *Collected Poems* was probably stimulated by the

17

feeling that the poem was too obviously a challenge to ideological abstracts.

8. *Ulysses* (1922) (New York, Modern Library, 1961), pp. 105–106. Other references to this edition will be found in the text. Bloom's thoughts follow a sententious remark by Mr. Kernan: *"I am the resurrection and the life. That touches a man's inmost heart."* (p. 105)

9. "Familiar," in *Selected Poems,* trans. Michael Hamburger and Christopher Middleton (New York, Harcourt Brace and World, n. d.), p. 26:

In unserem Museum,—wir besuchen es jeden Sonntag,—
hat man eine neue Abteilung eröffnet.
Unsere abgetriebenen Kinder, blasse, ernsthafte Embryos,
sitzen dort in schlichten Gläsern
und sorgen sich um die Zukunft ihrer Eltern.

10. In *Dependencies* (Chapel Hill, University of North Carolina Press, 1965), p. 12.

11. *The Disappearance of God* (Cambridge, Massachusetts, Harvard University Press, 1963), p. 1. Other references will be found in the text.

12. En haut, en bas, partout, la profondeur, la grève,
Le silence, l'espace affreux et captivant . . .
Sur le fond de mes nuits Dieu de son doigt savant
Dessine un cauchemar multiforme et sans trève.

Stanza 2 of "Le Gouffre," in *Oeuvres Completes,* ed. Y. G. Le Dantec (Paris, Gallimard, 1951), p. 242.

13. Quoted by Henri Poulet in *Studies in Human Time,* trans. Elliott Coleman (Baltimore, The Johns Hopkins University Press, 1956), p. 255.

14. In *Complete Poems and Plays* (New York, Harcourt Brace, 1952), p. 136; originally published in *The New English Weekly,* February 27, 1941.

15. *The Reign of Wonder* (Cambridge University Press, 1965), p. 9. See my review of this book, in *Shenandoah,* 17 (Winter, 1966), 106–110.

16. "Leda and the Swan" was written in 1923 and was

first published in *The Dial* of June, 1924, when Yeats was 59 years old. See *The Variorum Edition of the Poems* of W. B. Yeats, ed. Peter Allt and R. K. Allspach (New York, Macmillan, 1957), p. 441. Other references to this edition will be found in the text.

17. See Richard Ellmann, *The Identity of Yeats* (London, Macmillan, 1954), p. 39. "To hold certain ideas as 'beliefs' would give them a sort of autonomy; the mind, whose independence Yeats demanded, would become subservient to them, instead of their being necessary expressions of it."

18. "A New Poet," *Bookman,* 6 (August, 1894), 147–48; quoted in Ellmann, p. 43.

19. See *The Collected Poems of Wallace Stevens* (New York, Alfred Knopf, 1955), p. 92. Other references to this edition will be found in the text.

20. See "Anecdote of Men by the Thousand" (*Poems,* pp. 51–52) and "The Comedian as the Letter C" (pp. 27–46).

21. *Poems,* pp. 440–41, originally published 1948. The best book-length study of Stevens' poetry is Joseph N. Riddel's *The Clairvoyant Eye: The Poetry and Poetics of Wallace Stevens* (Baton Rouge, Louisiana State University Press, 1965); see especially ch. 6, "The World as Meditation," pp. 224–78.

THE HARDNESS OF REALITY:
JOYCE'S STEPHEN DEDALUS

1

I SHOULD LIKE TO BEGIN BY POINTING OUT CERTAIN
facts, whose significance will, I hope, later become
apparent. James Joyce was born February 2, 1882,
in Dublin. In 1904, when he was twenty-two years
old, he began writing a manuscript he called *Stephen
Hero*. In 1907 he gave up writing it, after having
produced more than nine hundred pages. Shortly
thereafter he began the revision (or the new version)
of the book, which was ultimately to become *A Portrait of the Artist as a Young Man,* published in
1916. Among other differences between the two versions of the Dedalus story is the fact that the hero's
name was simplified from Daedalus. In 1914 Joyce
began serious work on *Ulysses,* which was published
in 1922. This is the last of his works in which the
character Stephen Dedalus appears by that name,
but there is no doubt that "Shem the Penman" of
Finnegans Wake is a revival of him, in all but name.

The meaning of all of these facts has to do with
Joyce's relationship to Stephen Dedalus. At the beginning of his presentation of the Dedalus *imago,*
Joyce was only two years older than Stephen (a difference of twenty-two to twenty); at age twenty-five,
he decided to put more distance between himself and
his young hero. By the time *A Portrait* was published, there was a difference of twelve years, or the
ratio of thirty-four to twenty-two. This distance was
increased in *Ulysses;* Joyce was forty and Stephen
twenty-two, when that novel was published. To com-

21

plicate matters a bit further, he made Leopold Bloom thirty-eight, only two years younger than he was himself. In the creation of *Ulysses,* from 1914 to 1922, we may say that Joyce was treating of a contemporary in Leopold Bloom, but of a person of almost a later generation in Stephen. Yet in many respects that person was much like what Joyce *had been* when he was his age.

These matters are suggestive only. Joyce was close to *being* Stephen in the long, sprawling, embarrassingly close diary-novel, *Stephen Hero.* He undertook to disengage himself; and as he grew older and Stephen stayed the same age, the aesthetic values of distance began to accrue to Joyce's advantage. He exorcised the first Stephen by abandoning him (although part of the novel was actually published, some time after it could have mattered to Joyce's career); he treated the second with as much seriousness as the young man deserved, and Stephen grew to a point where he decided he should no longer grow; finally, in the character of Shem, the Stephen figure was more mocked than not. It isn't, of course, so simple as this account might suggest. But Joyce had two major tasks to perform: first, he needed to describe the revolt of a young man of the *fin de siècle* years (from 1890 to 1904) against his family, city, country, and church; and second, he needed to hold the drama of these events at a removal sufficiently great to judge them objectively.

2

The first impression one has of Stephen Dedalus in Joyce's *A Portrait of the Artist as a Young Man* (1916) is that of alternating darkness and light. There are accessory images: fire, warmth vs. slimy cold, and so forth. Gradually Stephen is inducted into the hard nature of reality; he is the young man walking in the dark into a doorpost, or being thrown into a cold slimy ditch:

> . . . He shivered as if he had cold slimy water next his skin. That was mean of Wells to shoulder him into the square ditch because he would not swop his little snuff-box for Wells's seasoned hacking chestnut. . . . How cold and slimy the water had been! A fellow had once seen a big rat jump into the scum. . . .[1]

The very young Stephen has a limited vocabulary with which to identify himself and to describe the dawning sense of an external reality, one not always available to rhetorical assuagement. He also comes to a shuddering realization of his own mortality. Chapter one of the *Portrait* is fairly and simply contained. The father figure (divided between Simon Dedalus and Mr. Casey) is still strong, and Stephen can still maneuver safely within the apparent certainties it offers—this despite the great Christmas dinner clash between religious and political certainties. It is only after his father has begun to fail as the "elegant provider" that Stephen begins his exploration of Dublin realities, or begins to "bump into"

them. The fire burning on the hearth no longer as-
sures him, and he is forced to move away from it.
Throughout he holds to the power of words, to explain reality or to stand in its place.

The changes in the family, "so many slight shocks
to his boyish conception of the world," (*Portrait,* p.
64) force him beyond himself and into the wider
range of Dublin life. He is still anxious, however, to
find a rhetoric that will stand satisfactorily in the
place of reality:

> . . . He wanted to meet in the real world the unsubstan-
> tial image which his soul so constantly beheld. He did
> not know where to seek it or how: but a premonition
> which led him on told him that this image would, with-
> out any overt act of his, encounter him. . . .
>
> (*Portrait,* p. 65)

The *Portrait* is the record of a succession of experiences and the search for appropriate rhetorics.
The "image" which will serve Stephen is indispensable to his receiving and tolerating reality; he has
been made aware of the dangers in a reality that is
not held at word's length. In the course of the novel,
three major rhetorical positions are made available
to him: that of the church; that of his romantic pose
as *fin de siècle* poet and man of letters; and the
aesthetic formulations made on the basis of what
elsewhere he calls "applied Aquinas." Stephen desperately needs *a* rhetoric at each stage of his growth.
His defiance of the Catholic morality when he engages a prostitute to alleviate both his desire and his

fear is returned to him in full force as the retreat sermons of chapter three convince him that he is guilty of the sins of adultery and of pride.

The Irish Catholic rhetoric is elaborate indeed.[2] It provides him with a vivid extension of his sin into an infinity and an eternity of punishment. The effect on him is to make him despair of his soul and cringe before the thought of death.

> . . . Time was to sin and to enjoy, time was to scoff at God and at the warnings of His holy church, time was to defy His majesty, to disobey His commands, to hoodwink one's fellow men, to commit sin after sin after sin and to hide one's corruption from the sight of men. But that time was over. Now it was God's turn: and He was not to be hoodwinked or deceived. . . .
>
> (*Portrait*, p. 112)

Stephen has always relied upon words, and is searching for the most suitable formulations of them. Now, however, words turn his soul inside out, expose its worst character to view, and offer speculations concerning the refinements of hell, both physical and spiritual. His almost inevitable reaction is to embrace the rhetoric of the Church. This Stephen does with a conscientiousness that makes him look as though he were following the rules in a handbook for novice saints.

To escape from an "eternity of endless agony, of endless bodily and spiritual torment," (*Portrait,* p. 133) he engages in a series of quotidian spiritual exercises. As Joyce says, "His daily life was laid out in devotional areas." (p. 147) And he does in fact work over the "manual" so exhaustively that he is bound eventually to wear it out and to become disillusioned as a result. As we proceed through chapter four of the *Portrait,* we can gradually sense the changeover in his temperament and in his spiritual disposition. So that when the Director of Studies asks him if he has had "a vocation" (p. 157), he cannot answer positively. A number of forces are working on him: on the one hand, he has found the exercises not adequate to his own powerful sense of dedication; but he does need an "established rite"— ". . . it was partly the absence of an appointed rite which had always constrained him to inaction whether he had allowed silence to cover his anger or pride or had suffered only an embrace he longed to give." (*Portrait,* p. 159) Some instinct, "subtle and hostile, . . . armed him against acquiescence. . . ." (p. 161)

In chapters four and five Stephen moves toward an aesthetic reordering of his life. At first there is the image of "dappled seaborne clouds," which ends in the secular emotional experience at the end of chapter four, and liberates him from the spiritual discipline. His experience is a composite of thoughts of Europe (from which the seaborne clouds had come), of himself as creator (the clever, cunning artificer, *Daidalos*), and of the purest kind of sensual experience. The light, delicate, yet frankly sensual detail suits his mood perfectly, and it helps to dispel the ugliness of the world of the prostitute at the end of chapter two. The experience is a "holy ecstasy"; it affects his soul and spurs him on to take risks with the life still at his disposal:

> . . . A wild angel had appeared to him, the angel of mortal youth and beauty, an envoy from the fair courts of life, to throw open before him in an instant of ecstasy the gates of all the ways of error and glory. . . .
>
> (*Portrait,* p. 172)

This is the reaction of the late nineteenth century, of Yeats' first poems; it is primarily a rhetoric of youth, and it is to lead to an aesthetic reformulation of his purpose and vocation. Stephen will apparently emerge at the end of the *Portrait* a self-sustaining person, who knows what he wants to do and has a new rhetoric to explain it to himself and to his contemporaries. In a sense this truth about him makes the progress of the *Portrait* convincingly real; his experiences are enfolded within a succession of styles that penetrate close to the center of his ego. The much quoted and debated phrases of chapter five (the phrases from Saint Thomas's *Summa*) are not nearly so important as is the explanatory continuity of styles, which define Stephen at each stage of his growth. It is a progress from simplicity to a degree of complexity, but no one can claim that Stephen has found an "ultimate resolution" according to which he will be able to live flawlessly and without accident.

The fact is that reality still protrudes. Words, stances, points-of-view do not satisfactorily conceal it or make it harmless. In the opening three episodes of *Ulysses,* Stephen's position as the preoccupied intellectual, the poet, the bullock-befriending bard, is even more precarious than it appears at the end of the *Portrait.* There *is* no entirely satisfactory way of accounting for reality at any given moment. Stephen's rebellion against the Church has not been whole-hearted or final; he is aware still of its mysteries, its elaborate strategies of explanation, its possibly eventual "rightness." If we can accept Shem the Penman as the nearest equivalent of Stephen in *Finnegans Wake,* we must admit that Joyce has become more and more objective about the young man who in *Stephen Hero* was so close to Joyce as to cause him embarrassment.

> . . . (who meanwhile, with increasing lack of interest in his semantics, allowed various subconscious smickers to drivel slowly across their fichers), unconsciously explaining, for inkstands, with a meticulosity bordering on the insane, the various meanings of all the different foreign parts of speech he misused and cuttlefishing every lie unshrinkable about all the other people in the story, leaving out, of course, foreconsciously, the simple worf and plague and poison they had cornered him about until there was not a snoozer among them but was utterly undeceived in the heel of the reel by the recital of the rigmarole.[3]

3

At the disposal of so many different types of rhetorical explanation, Stephen Dedalus has undergone an experience which all but identifies the twentieth century and him with it. Any number of generalizations are possible concerning his intellectual role. It is on the one hand an ordinary tale of "growing up," but only in a very limited, literal sense. I should like to use it as the starting-off place for the development of a thesis: that a young man's encounter with reality in the twentieth-century experience has been immensely complicated, and that he has himself aided in the process through a deliberate act of shifting allegiances. In short, there are both a subjective and an objective complexity in the adjustment of rhetoric to reality. The pressure of the sciences, the heavy factual weight upon natural explanation, constitutes the more obvious aspect of the situation.

Joyce's story is especially effective because the *Portrait* moves into a steadily increasing complexity and abstraction of reference. Stephen at first interprets experiences in a basically simple way; the implication is that he does not need more than the authorities of church and home to protect him from reality. They are, in other words, fully acceptable and useful. But exceptions occur to their usefulness, and Stephen on several occasions has to improvise meanings in order to escape chaos. Ultimately he *chooses* to live the life of the exile and—having assumed the position of the non-Catholic and ex-Dubliner—returns in his imagination to give the reality of Dublin a strong, dense, and profound rhetorical treatment and embellishment. To offer a variation upon Richard Ellmann's figure, Joyce stamped angrily out of the house, slamming the door, then quietly moved around to a window and looked in— at himself angrily leaving and slamming the door. Stephen's pride in the *non-serviam* gesture at the novel's conclusion is a genuine one, the more so because of its involving certain responsibilities as artist, moral man, and personality; in reply to Cranly's question whether he fears punishment for his apostasy, Stephen says:

> . . . I fear more than that the chemical action which would be set up in my soul by a false homage to a symbol behind which are massed twenty centuries of authority and veneration.
>
> (*Portrait,* p. 243)

Of course, he has to suffer the consequences of his decision. Through *Ulysses* and *Finnegans Wake* we discover Joyce debating the legitimacy of the young artist's rebellion against one set of authorities. But the principal importance of Joyce's artist as a young man is stylistic. The questions he struggles to answer have to do with: (a) the consequences of a free decision, and (b) the treacherous and difficult reality he must face and comprehend alone and without assistance. Joyce is the man who is making the decisions, but the language of the decisions is given to Stephen, to Leopold Bloom, and to H. C. Earwicker.

Most important, the crisis is one of comprehending reality with a style that is sufficiently rich and elaborate and complex to make it acceptable outside the scope of traditionally feasible systems of explanation. We all know that Joyce's style became increasingly complex. The very first stories and sketches, published in the *Irish Homestead,* are simpler than the versions published in *Dubliners.* The *Portrait* is a less cluttered and a much more subtle book than *Stephen Hero.* Although the early episodes of *Ulysses* marked a decisive experimental advance in twentieth-century fiction, they are much less complex than the boldly and consciously intricate final episodes. Even so, the versions published in *The Little Review* and *The Egoist* from 1918 to 1920 were revised and "enriched" for their place in the 1922 first edition of *Ulysses.*[4]

These enlargements and elaborations have more than a mere historical significance. Perhaps it is risking too much oversimplification to state the reasons as Walton Litz has, but some variant of his explanation appears to be in order.

> . . . . In the second and third decades of this century our greatest artists found the inherited forms of communications unsuited to their new visions, and began to experiment with more radical techniques. At the centre of this experimentation lay the doctrine of the "Image," an aesthetic concept which illuminates Joyce's mature methods.[5]

The "doctrine of the 'Image' " can help us to see Joyce's development in a technical sense, but it might be more important to look into *what* Joyce added, how he responded to contemporary influences, and just in what ways style was associated with the intellectual history of the times.

In fact, Joyce approached the religious crisis in two different ways. He began writing *Stephen Hero* in 1904, and he apparently had more than nine hundred pages of manuscript by the time when, in 1907, he decided to change his approach to the subject. The approach of *Stephen Hero* was very much like that of Stanislaus Joyce's *My Brother's Keeper*, full of the minor particulars, all but inhibited by too much undifferentiated detail, and dominated by bitterness toward Dublin, the Church, and the Joyce family. Joyce did not do much more than assert his oppositions and document them. The decision to change his perspective corresponded to his deepening awareness that the relationship of religion and reality is immensely complex and could not be set aside in an easy, forensic way. The *Portrait* is therefore a much more carefully thought out and a much more "aware" work of art. The reality of the exile and the renegade and his reasons for leaving his faith and his native city were in need of a more subtle treatment than it had received in *Stephen Hero*.

The growth in complexity was not just a matter of Joyce's having taken advantage of the "doctrine of the 'Image.' " Joyce began to improvise with styles as early as some of the stories in *Dubliners*. The primary substance of his experiment was the mundane, the commonplace world, to which he wished to point as the source of courage and humanity. The heroics of Joyce's world were humdrum; the rhetoric of Bloom's "facticity" takes over from that of Stephen's elaborate posing; and in the total economy of *Ulysses,* it is the commonplace hero who shines in comparison with the young artist elaborating upon his *non-serviam* gesture. As a result *Ulysses* is, superficially, a chaos. Joyce needs some seven hundred eighty-three pages to describe slightly over eighteen hours of an ordinary day in Dublin. He is attempting here to assert what he has Stephen exclaim at the end of chapter four of the *Portrait:* the simplicity and the naturalness of human relationships.

Throughout Joyce's career it is Stephen who seeks for elaborate formulas of explanation, for the purpose not so much of understanding reality as of controlling it. He is puzzled and bemused by the spectacle of manifold being, and he seeks to account for it by his erudition and the ingenuity of his mind.

> . . . My soul walks with me, form of forms, he says to himself in Ulysses. So in the moon's midwatches I pace the path above the rocks, in sable silvered, hearing Elsinore's tempting flood.[7]

4

In one essential way, Joyce's opting for Bloom's mind over Stephen's is characteristic of our times. This does not mean that modern writers prefer the reductively simple explanation to the tortured and difficult one; it simply points to what Pound called "accuracy" in writing:

> Roughly then, good writing is writing that is perfectly

controlled, the writer says just what he means. He says it with complete clarity and simplicity. . . . granting that two sentences are at times easier to understand than one sentence containing the double meaning, the author tries to communicate with the reader with the greatest possible despatch, save where for any one of forty reasons he does not wish to do so.[8]

Much of the complexity of modern style comes from modern conditioning; Stephen's emergence in chapter 5 of the *Portrait* as a theoretician of the arts is a natural and a typical development. He has given up one way of comprehending reality, and he must choose another and remain responsible to it.

The aesthetic of *Portrait* is itself an adaptation from the metaphysics of Saint Thomas Aquinas. Other ventures of Joyce involved literary adaptations of non-literary thought to a reality that needed comprehension. The importance of Giambattista Vico to *Finnegans Wake* is a case in point. As Rudolph Bultmann has said of Vico's theory of history, "The idea of eschatology, of a goal and consummation of history, is eliminated by Vico's understanding of the historical development. For, according to him, the course of history is a cyclical one, running in the rhythm of *corso and ricorso* (course and recurrence). . . ."[9] *Finnegans Wake* demonstrates this rhythm of *corso and ricorso* from the start.

Stephen's experience may be said to represent many such adventures. It is not clearly understood whether the meditative world of the priesthood fails him or if he fails it; in any case, he assumes (as did

Joyce with him) the task of revaluating the sum and substance of his experience. This requires his living and working in terms of Beckett's "absolute absence of the Absolute."[10] It also means that Joyce's work will be invaded by the "relative," swamped by the "quotidian," charged with the special wit of the mundane. Wallace Stevens speaks of a similar situation in "The Comedian as the Letter C." (1923) Crispin, his hero, decides to scrap all "mental moonlight," all lex, "Rex and principium . . .":

> Hence the reverberations in the words
> Of his first central hymns, the celebrants
> Of rankest trivia, tests of the strength
> Of his aesthetic, his philosophy,
> The more invidious, the more desired:[11]

In short, Crispin allows the quotidian to inundate him; he has assumed the role of rankest realist. Yet while the task of annotating reality, of serving "Grotesque apprenticeship to chance event," seems momentarily desirable, the process is far too simplistic; and Crispin ends by realizing that "the quotidian saps philosophers," and

> For all it takes it gives a humped return
> Exchequering from piebald fiscs unkeyed.[12]

There are risks, of course, in all attempts to serve directly as an annotator of reality. Form and style are necessary to qualify it, to prevent a veritable flood and waste of life from taking over. The "hardness of reality" is in short a composite of its many qualities: its abundance, its resistance to attempts formally to contain or define it, its sharp angularities, and generally its survival of improvisatory definitions.

There is no doubt that Stephen is aware of the gravity of his choice, and he does not make the mistakes of Stevens' Crispin; he remains, after all, within reach of the great doctors of the Church. In reply to Cranly, who asks if he intends to become a Protestant, he says, "I said that I had lost the faith, . . . but not that I had lost self-respect. What kind of liberation would that be to foresake an absurdity which is logical and coherent and to embrace one which is illogical and incoherent?" (*Portrait,* pp. 243–244) He respects above all the great powers of formulation residing in the Church, but he will insist upon the privilege of barking his own shins against the sharp edges of reality.

5

Joyce is so intensely "within" his creations, and his use of Dublin and its various institutions is apparently so accurate, that one has a tendency to assume that he and Stephen are equivalent.[13] No one, so the argument goes, could have realized a world so vividly if he had not been identified closely with it. There is no doubt that Joyce came closer to actuality in his fiction than almost any other artist of modern literature. But there are degrees of separation as well, and Joyce's freedom from actual involvement in the affairs of his creatures must be accepted. It is not that the world of his fiction has no relation to him. Rather, Joyce's initial intensity (the raw anger, hatred, and distress that showed all too plainly in the young man of 1902 through 1904) modified as he matured. He was, in one sense at least, able to "conquer his world by naming it"; and the power of language in his work is undeniable. Beyond this skill, there was his great talent for representing himself in figures who were other than he, removed from him by distance and time both. There is no way of proving such a statement as the following by R. P. Blackmur, but it is a fascinating insight, that of Joyce's "working out the polarities of his nature [Bloom and Stephen] in terms of the breakdown of the Christian world as he actually experienced it in his youth."[14] Blackmur's contention is that Joyce somehow distributed his early experiences and that the actual artist lies somewhere between the creations of Stephen and Bloom.

This is pure speculation, and the errors both of omission and commission in Joyce criticism are sufficiently weird; they don't need adding to.[15] I can only point to a number of facts. Joyce did suffer from great disillusionment and anger in his native Dublin, and he did use voluntary exile as the first means both of expressing and of purging his emotions. Once permanently exiled from Dublin, however,[16] he returned to it in his imagination. There is no doubt that he was able to illuminate the world

37

of Dublin with far greater skill after he had left it. The Stephen Daedalus of *Stephen Hero* frequently has the appearance of a character observed directly from the actual and set down almost without any aesthetic revaluation. Psychologically, so much energy went into Joyce's *being* angry, indignant, scornful, and so forth, that there was little left for his being the "cunning" artificer he later became. Not only nine years elapsed between his abandonment of the *Stephen Hero* manuscript and the serious work of the *Portrait;* he had also written most of the *Dubliners* stories, and his experiments with relatively simple symbolic extensions of his experience had been "got out of the way." Stephen Dedalus of the *Portrait* and Stephen and Bloom of *Ulysses* are consequently creations of a much more talented, a more removed, and a less gullible Joyce. Ironies play upon the excesses of each. In Stephen's case they are Joyce's ironies all but invariably; in Bloom, Joyce masterfully created a person who was able both to *be* and ironically to reflect upon the attitudes he assumes.

The major fact is that of Joyce's separation from the great influences of his youth. Kristan Smidt puts it in this way:

> Joyce not only feared that Christianity might be true, he felt intimately that behind the Christian symbols there "are massed twenty centuries of authority and veneration." The forces which held him back and tied him to home and tradition were extremely powerful ones, and he did not just discard his faith as he might have cast

aside a worn shirt. He obviously fought for it as he fought for his freedom from it. In the process he was at least convinced of possessing a spiritual soul, and the conviction was always to colour his thoughts and vocabulary.[17]

I should like to interpret Joyce's position in terms of the aesthetic distribution of emotional energies. To the end of the *Portrait* Stephen has things his own way, for the most part. There is only a brief glimpse of what in *Ulysses* is to dominate him by way of guilt feelings. The initial stages of his rebellion are effectively given, but limited deliberately in their nature. Stephen has scarcely done anything that may be said to lead to a full moral consequence; even the decision to confess his sins and to turn to the life of the Church is prompted by a painful need to rid himself of fear, to relieve himself of bad dreams.

The Stephen of the *Portrait* is heroic only in a limited sense. The decision to act on his own initiative and to refuse established answers to deeply personal questions has a dignity of a kind, but it must be seen in terms of Stephen's own limited experience. The perspective upon him in *Ulysses* has become that of the artist judging a limited person who may in some respects have been himself, years ago. The important new factor in *Ulysses* is Bloom, Ulysses himself, a person of limited sophistication, but also one whose capacity to love and to "save" are immensely enhanced. Bloom is by no means a superior figure; he is, in fact, gauche, tiresome, troublesome, and clumsy. But he is, above all, *humane,* and he is also frequently aware of his own limitations and able to reflect comically upon them. The rhetorics of the two—the young (22) Irish poet, the middle-aged (38) Jew-in-Dublin—provide a constant and a stimulating series of meditations on life as a whole, on the relation of decision-making to "growing up," on the consequences (immediate and final) of personal and moral decisions. Any number of contrasting examples are available. The following two are representative: in the first, from the "Proteus" chapter, Stephen, alone except for the sea and the corpse of a dog, speculates upon himself as if he were not really fleshed; in the second, from "The Lestrygonians," Bloom locates his humanity within the context of humanity in general but never loses his identity as a special commentator upon the fallible human condition:

> Stephen closed his eyes to hear his boots crush crackling wrack and shells. You are walking through it howsomever. I am, a stride at a time. A very short space of time through very short times of space. Five, six: *nacheinander.* Exactly: and that is the ineluctable modality of the audible. Open your eyes. Ho. Jesus! If I fell over a cliff that beetles o'er his base, fell through the *nebeneinander* ineluctably. I am getting on nicely in the dark. . . .
> (*Ulysses,* p. 37)

Stephen here emphasizes his separation from life by closing his eyes and using his ashplant as a "reality measure." The passage is Aristotelian, as Stephen sees the Aristotle of *De Anima* in relation to himself, and there is a quotation from Hamlet in it as well. His major preoccupation, throughout the day of *Ulysses,* is with human entanglement, but his concern is not to look at them humanely but to appeal to literature and philosophy as means of avoiding a personal involvement in them. The *Hamlet* context provides him with an elaborate rationalization of his human failure. The discussion of space and time is a temporary attempt to "lock himself into" the abstract worlds of space and time. The passage is almost a paradigm of self-isolation and self-indulgence.

Bloom's thoughts, which occur as he is looking for a place for luncheon, are much more universally meaningful, yet they identify Bloom as a person more exactly as well:

> His smile faded as he walked, a heavy cloud hiding the sun slowly, shadowing Trinity's surly front. Trams passed one another, ingoing, outgoing, clanging. Useless words. Things go on same; day after day: squads of police marching out, back: trams in, out. Those two loonies mooching about. Dignam carted off. Mina Purefoy swollen belly on a bed groaning to have a child tugged out of her. One born every second somewhere. Other dying every second. Since I fed the birds five minutes. Three hundred kicked the bucket. Other three hundred born, washing the blood off, all washed in the blood of the lamb, bawling maaaaa.
>
> (*Ulysses,* p. 164)

The details of Bloom's day are explicitly there, but they are located within a context that is in turn

41

farcical and profound. During the day of *Ulysses* Bloom will have attended both to life and to death, and he will also have suffered several insults to his person, not the least of them self-inflicted. Bloom is always saved from being, or even seeming, heroic because his reflections never cease being at least partially comic. He has long since passed the time when merely to make a decision was glamorous or heroic, and he now has mainly to "abide"—that is, to "care and not to care." His reaction to life is a "sizing up." Moral judgments and philosophical generalities never entirely escape being somewhat comic, partly because he is not a man to strike an heroic pose and partly because he is aware of his own absurdity. It is this awareness of himself as a paltry, time-ridden, death-bound human that endows his position with dignity, in spite of himself.

6

In one of the better studies of *Ulysses,* S. L. Goldberg, commenting upon the general issue of Joyce's rebellion against Ireland and Rome, makes this shrewd remark:

> . . . Faced with the absolute and comprehensive claims of Roman Catholicism—claims the force of which he had experienced in the very moulding of his sensibility— he had to work out the grounds for his own moral activity as a man and an artist with a compensating absoluteness and comprehensiveness.[18]

Goldberg continues in this vein, dismissing the too easy notion that Joyce simply tried to substitute a religion of art for another set of religious values; art was for him, instead, "the engagement, discovery and enactment of those values; but the context in which he was forced to establish his attitude led him to take all life as his personal province, to aspire to contain more than he could in fact actually and fully grasp, and to employ artistic methods that falsified his own proper insights."

If there is something negative in Goldberg's summing up, it is because he thinks Joyce gave up too much—in the second half of *Ulysses* and in *Finnegans Wake*—of his truly comic and realistic powers in the interest of being elaborately clever, as well as of satisfying the need "to comprehend his society whole and to judge it." (p. 302) The critical truth is there: Joyce's greatest decision was that of substituting one mode for another, one context for another. The world was as large and as complex after his decision as it was before it. He was so deeply influenced by the training he received, from Dublin and from the Church, that he proceeded to represent his world with a scrupulous regard for the niceties of moral necessity and human imperfection. He became, in fact, his own Jesuit, judging both practically and morally, never very far away from the actual rituals of the Church, always compensating (in the sense of "allowing") for losses in insight and terminology incurred through his separation from it.

In these circumstances, it is obvious that Joyce

could not long abide with Stephen Dedalus. It is
not only that Stephen was a twenty-two-year-old
Joyce, observed by a thirty-five or forty-year-old
Joyce, or that Joyce needed to "purge" Stephen before he could move on to more mature work.[19] It is
also naïve to think that Joyce caused Leopold to exercise a strong though mysterious influence over
Stephen.[20] Joyce expanded his comprehension of
humanity as he perfected the means of representing
it in art. He kept his sights upon his own personal
experience of comprehending it; both Dublin and
Irish Catholicism grew in his retrospective analysis
of it. Stephen's clash with reality, his recoiling from
the experience, and his attempt to remake the framework of his understanding, were a part of Joyce's
ultimate fable of sinning man. But Joyce believed
that he needed a different, a more complicated, and
a more forgiving nature to set against that of Stephen. The exile in Dublin, the Jew in search of a
son, the cuckold, the man with a thousand timely
hints on how to live with human imperfections and
how to tolerate life: these images put Stephen, as
they put Joyce, within a remarkable world that is
gross, comical, and tragic, by turns, and ends by
being tolerable, though perhaps just barely so.

NOTES

1. *A Portrait of the Artist as a Young Man* (New York,
Compass Books, 1964), p. 10. Other references to this edition will be found in the text.

The Hardness of Reality

2. It is really a nineteenth-century rhetoric. See James R. Thrane, "Joyce's Sermon on Hell: Its Source and Its Backgrounds," *Modern Philology,* 57 (February, 1960), 172–98.

3. *Finnegans Wake* (New York, Viking Press, 1939), pp. 173–74. This appears in the "Shem the Penman" section, directly before the famous "Anna Livia Plurabelle" pages, which (along with other and later passages) affirm sex, motherhood, being, in terms equivalent though not like those of the end of *Ulysses.*

4. Of the approximately twenty-five changes from the version of episode one published in *The Little Review* of March, 1918, three-fourths are additions. The significant changes have to do with Stephen's troubles of conscience and his rebellion against Ireland and the faith. On page 14 of the most recent edition (1961), Stephen, reflecting bitterly upon women, thinks: "To the voice that will shrive and oil for the grave all there is of her but her woman's unclean loins. . . ." The book version has added: ". . . . of man's flesh made not in God's unlikeness, the serpent's prey." Twice the Anglo-Saxon phrase, *Agenbite of inwit,* is added to the early text, the first rather elaborately: "Speaking to me. They wash and tub and scrub, Agenbite of inwit, Conscience. Yet here's a spot." (p. 16) Near the end, Stephen muses upon the growth of his own religious views: ". . . the slow growth and change of rite and dogma like his own rare thoughts, a chemistry of stars." (p. 21) Everything suggests the fact that Joyce was anxious to link Stephen's thoughts more closely to his conscience, troubled by his rebellion against the Church and his refusal to kneel at his mother's bedside.

5. *The Art of James Joyce* (London, Oxford University Press, 1961), p. 53.

6. Edited by Richard Ellmann (New York, Viking Press, 1958). At the time of Stanislaus' death in 1955, his account of his brother had been brought to the twenty-second year.

7. *Ulysses* (New York, Random House, 1961), p. 44.

Other references to this edition will be found in the text.

8. "The Serious Artist" (1913), in *Pavannes and Divisions* (New York, Alfred Knopf, 1918), p. 233.

9. *History and Eschatology* (New York, Harper and Brothers, 1957), p. 65.

10. "Dante, Bruno, Vico, Joyce," in *Our Exagmination Round His Factification for Incamination of Work in Progress* (New York, New Directions, 1962, p. 22); originally published in Paris by Shakespeare and Company in 1929.

11. *Collected Poems* (New York, Alfred Knopf, 1955), p. 37; originally published in *Harmonium,* 1923.

12. *Ibid.,* pp. 39, 42, 43.

13. See the remarkable performance of Kristan Smidt, in *James Joyce and the Cultic Use of Fiction* (Oxford, Blackwell, 1955). Almost all of the distortions in this book come from the author's making little distinction between an author and his creations.

14. "The Jew in Search of a Son," *Virginia Quarterly Review,* 24 (Winter, 1948), 115.

15. Rudolph von Abele lists most of them in *"Ulysses:* The Myth of Myth," *PMLA,* 59 (June, 1954), 358–64. Among the more interesting speculations are the identification of Stephen, Bloom, and Molly with various types of mythic figures. One critic, Edward Duncan, identifies Stephen with Christ as the "Paschal Lamb, who recapitulates Christ's temptation in the desert, and finally suffers a symbolic death at the hand of the soldiers. . . ." (p. 359)

16. He was called back from Paris in 1903, then left for the Continent with Nora Barnacle in October of 1904; he returned for visits five times, but Europe (Trieste, Zurich, and Paris) was his real home after the break in 1904.

17. *James Joyce and the Cultic Use of Fiction,* p. 25.

18. *The Classical Temper: A Study of James Joyce's "Ulysses"* (New York, Barnes and Noble, 1961), p. 302. Other references to this book are given in the text.

19. For this latter position, see Hugh Kenner, *Dublin's*

Joyce (Bloomington, Indiana University Press, 1956), especially ch. 8, pp. 109–133.

20. For a statement concerning this view, see Stanley Sultan, *The Argument of Ulysses* (Columbus, The Ohio State University Press, 1964), especially pp. 345–55.

THE FRIENDS OF GOD:

DOSTOEVSKY AND KAZANTZAKIS

1

THE TITLE OF THIS LECTURE REQUIRES SOME EX-
planation. It is derived from a rather complex set
of ideas, discussed briefly in my first lecture. They
involve, first, the notion that there was a gradual
change from objective to subjective grounds in the
analysis of creation; that is, that man, from accept-
ing an objective world in which God (who had created him) existed, ultimately thought of himself as
the creator of the *idea* of God (who therefore joined
the subjective world within the mind of man). Second, there is the subsequent assumption by man of
a sense of responsibility, or concern, over the position and merits of a transcendent Being within a
solely subjective world which was created by man
and must therefore be sustained by him. Dostoevsky,
Kazantzakis, and any number of other writers are
the "friends of God" in the sense that they must sustain Him within the same subjective universe they
themselves inhabit.

Either God is created by man, and therefore is a
subjective phenomenon, or He does not—and cannot—exist. This is an idea that carries with it nu-
merous imaginative possibilities. The necessity to
endure is seen in many speculative contexts, from
Faulkner to Beckett. The latter most frequently has
his characters, in plays and novels, puzzle themselves, first over the nature of the universe (which
they cannot see), second over their own natures
(which diminish before our very eyes), and third

over the likelihood of a God's existing who has or may have some influence over them. Although these problems beset all of Beckett's characters, they are shown as especially active in *Waiting for Godot*. (1952) There is only occasionally speculation about the Christ figure (it is mentioned two or three times in *Godot*); but in the sense of man's sole responsibility to and for the divine agency, Beckett's novels and plays abound in this kind of speculation.[1]

2

Among both first-rank and lesser writers, the "imagination's new beginning" sometimes takes the form of wishing to befriend the deity, for reasons I have just discussed. The argument runs this way: because of man's contradictoriness, his proclivity for evil, and his frequent preference for the worst distortions of virtue, God needs considerable assistance if He is going to tolerate them or to hide His embarrassment over the botch of creation for which He seems responsible. The drama of the Incarnation is, of course, the key instance of God's accommodation to man. It is also the one event stared at with wonder, and puzzlement, and alarm, by artists who regard the Christian drama and doctrine responsibly. There is no doubt that they are frequently more fascinated by the terror and distortion caused by Christ's physical suffering than by any doctrinal justification of His "funding" the sources of Grace and making them available to the active Christian.

One of the more startling examples of man's interest in and dread over the tight battle between humanity and divinity occurred in the circumstances of Dostoevsky's writing *The Idiot* (1869). In her reminiscences, his wife has described his terrified fascination in Basel, Switzerland, as he stared at the Holbein painting of Christ in the tomb.[2]

> He stood for twenty minutes before the picture without moving. On his agitated face there was the frightened expression I often noticed on it during the first moments of his epileptic fits. He had no fit at the time, but he could never forget the sensation he had experienced in the Basel museum in 1867: the figure of Christ taken from the cross, whose body already showed signs of decomposition, haunted him like a horrible nightmare. In his notes to *The Idiot* and in the novel itself he returns again and again to this theme.[3]

The Idiot is one of the great works in the modern history of religious doubt. It is not, however, unique in Dostoevsky's canon (there are many other examples of his genuine concern over the validity and reliability of divine symbols and characters); nor can we say that the story is really a story of Christ. Yet there are many suggestions concerning Prince Myshkin's role in his creator's religious meditation. Romano Guardini calls Myshkin a symbol of Christ and offers this summary of his meaning:

> . . . Myshkin is not the God-Man, or a second Christ. He is a man with a name, Lyov Nikolayev Myshkin. His

existence is made up of purely human elements: body
and soul, sorrow and joy, his inheritance and his poverty,
his luck and his catastrophe. But from his human existence, the image arises of another existence which is not
human, that of the Man-God.[4]

There are several reasons for Prince Myshkin. For
one thing, throughout his career Dostoevsky suffered
from a great fear of death, or at least a disturbance
of his faith concerning the religious assurances con-
nected with death and the hereafter. Also, he consciously and ambitiously sought to portray the "good
man," thought for a while of Don Quixote,[5] then
turned to Christ himself, the only example, he
claimed, of the "positively good man."[6] There is the
obvious interest that the Christ figure holds for anyone of Dostoevsky's disposition: the great chasm
between doubt and acceptance concerning the Incarnation, in which doubt is encouraged by the fear
that Christ's humanity will shunt off His divinity.
Christ becomes a test case. It is not He who fails
man; rather, man's obvious perverseness, and his
many reasons for not *deserving* the rewards of the
Incarnation, make Dostoevsky wonder if no one is
immune from the disaster of assuming the physical
character and the moral risks of being human.

Dostoevsky was very much aware of these terrible
human weaknesses, but he was above all fascinated
by the extremes of idealism and bestiality, of honesty
and cunning, of which man is capable. The childlike
figure of Myshkin did not occur to him until the fifth
of eight plans that he made for the novel. Myshkin

is first described in his *Notebooks* in this way:

> Pure, beautiful, worthy, stern, very nervous, deeply Christian, and compassionately loving. . . . There is no profundity or arrogance in his ideas, although he is wise, educated, and a thinker. But feeling predominates in his nature. He lives for feeling. He lives powerfully and passionately. In one word, his nature is Christian.[7]

Myshkin's honesty, depth of feeling, strength of foreboding, and purity of heart are designed to characterize him as the Christ image. But Dostoevsky uses him primarily as a test figure, who enacts Dostoevsky's own fears and doubts. *The Idiot* is therefore an ambitious experiment concerned with the survival power of the "positively good man," the simple and pure man, in a world inhabited by persons much more given to self-indulgence, much more devious and cunning and selfish, than he.

That this is no idle or trivial maneuvering with the nature of man is testified by Dostoevsky's friendship with the Russian philosopher, Vladimir Solovyev. When Solovyev was a lecturer in philosophy at Moscow University, he worked out his theory regarding the immanence of God in man. The central thesis is that the Godhood is manifested in man, that man is the test of the Incarnation.[8] Dostoevsky was personally and passionately interested in this question. In a letter to another friend, Nicolai Fyodorov, he expressed one of several doubts and fears, that concerning the resurrection of man:

> . . . you don't explain how you understand this resurrec-

tion of our ancestors and in what form you imagine and believe it will come about. Do you understand it allegorically as Renan does? . . . There must be a reply to this question, for otherwise everything will be incomprehensible. I must warn you that we here, that is, Solovyov and I, at any rate, believe in real, literal, personal resurrection and that it will come to pass on earth.[9]

These evidences, and much more, point to Dostoevsky's personal concern over the Incarnation and over Christ's power to transcend the weaknesses of man and to allow his divinity to survive his "adventure in humanity." Arrogance in these matters puzzled and outraged him. Yet, as in the case of Alyosha and Father Zossima, in *The Brothers Karamazov,* the horrible doubt remained: does blessedness, does even divinity, survive the death of man? In the concluding scene of *The Idiot,* the hovering fly is menacingly suspended above the corpse that has only recently been the beautiful Nastasya Filippovna:

> . . . On the little table at the head of the bed diamonds, which had been taken off and thrown down, lay glittering. At the foot of the bed some sort of lace lay in a crumpled heap, and on the white lace, protruding from under the sheet, the tip of a bare foot could be made out; it seemed as though it were carved out of marble, and it was dreadfully still. The prince looked, and he felt that the longer he looked the more still and death-like the room became. Suddenly a fly, awakened from its sleep, started buzzing, and after flying over the bed, settled at the head of it. The prince gave a start.

> (*Idiot,* p. 652)

3

Myshkin brings to his experiences several extra-ordinary traits: a childlike simplicity, an intensity of moral vision, a depth of concern over his fellows. He is also sensitive beyond human powers to evil, prospective and retrospective. Early in the novel, looking at Nastasya's portrait with an unusual intensity, "He seemed anxious to solve some mystery that was hidden in that face and that had struck him before. . . ." It is a face of great beauty, but there is much suffering in it as well. (*Idiot,* pp. 107–108) Myshkin's interest in it is largely a matter of exploring the possibilities inherent in man for contravening his own chance of salvation, an almost neurotic persistence in sinfulness and a fear of goodness. Myshkin's awareness of these perverse traits goes with spiritual insights, the effect of which is to distress and to frighten him. Superficially, he does not understand human depravity, or would prefer to remain immune from its effects; yet, not only does it exist, but he is more aware of its existence and its possibility than is any of his contemporaries. In his contemplation of Nastasya's portrait, he sees in her face the source of future sufferings and dangers: ". . . the very sight of her face on the portrait made his heart overflow with agonizing pity; the feeling of compassion and even of torment for this woman never left his heart and it had not left it now." (*Idiot,* p. 386)

Myshkin's tenure in the world of men depends

upon two conditions: his ability to tolerate wickedness, and man's willingness to restrain his own desire to commit sin. It is at best a tenuous affair, and ultimately he is stricken by the "idiocy" which had originally given him his nickname. He is reduced by Nastasya's death to silence and total noncomprehension.

> . . . The prince was sitting motionless beside [Rogozhin] on the cushions, and every time the sick man burst out screaming or began rambling, he hastened to pass his trembling hand gently over his hair and cheeks, as though caressing and soothing him. But he no longer understood the questions he was asked, and did not recognize the people who had come into the room and surrounded him. And if Schneider[10] himself had come from Switzerland now to have a look at his former pupil and patient, remembering the condition in which the prince had sometimes been during the first year of his treatment in Switzerland, he would have given him up with a despairing wave of a hand and would have said, as he did then: "An idiot!"
>
> (*Idiot*, p. 657)

At this point it appears that Myshkin has finally been overcome by evil, that Rogozhin, in murdering Nastasya, had finally convinced him of the irrevocable nature of man's proclivity toward evil. Dostoevsky appears to have put him to the ultimate test, and he has failed.[11] But he has meanwhile, in his sometimes ludicrous but always admonitory presence, called his friends' attention to themselves. He is the kind of modern personality who draws sinners compulsively toward a confessional act (like Conrad's

Marlow and Fitzgerald's Carraway and Dick Diver).
For him, they appear willing to confide, to confess,
and to listen to counsel. Because he is Dostoevsky's
creation, his thoughts are often on the themes of
death and execution, on the relationship of time
and eternity, on evil and the consequences in eternity of its commission. Two major scenes haunt the
novel throughout: that of an execution (whether
carried out or stopped at the last moment) and that
of the Holbein Christ, all too visibly human, being
laid in his tomb (the death before the resurrection,
when all is thrown into doubt and confusion). Myshkin provides a perspective on both. In the early
chapters he tells the story of an execution and another about a criminal reprieved. When he is asked
by Aglaya Yepanchin about a subject for a painting,
he suggests that she paint "the face of a condemned
man a minute before the fall of the guillotine
blade. . . ." The prisoner has been waiting an eternity for this moment; his face will be like that of
Christ in the Basel painting. (*Idiot,* pp. 90–91)

This dreadful scene is drawn from Dostoevsky's
own experience. He had been arrested, in April of
1849, and on December 22 he and his fellows were
taken from prison, apparently to be shot. All of the
details of the execution were carried out, except the
last; and no one was informed until the last minute
of a reprieve.[12] The memory of this experience
stayed with him all his life, and it is graphically
represented by the Prince. The crucial moment is the
moment before death, and especially if the death

57

is "staged," as in an execution. What can possibly avail man in a situation like this? Will not all of his faith in universals desert him? Won't the corruptibility of the flesh in death be the sole impression we have left? These questions dominate Dostoevsky's novel. It is interesting to see how often he struggles with them in all of his work. The sins of his characters are met either by suicide (which is always described in a frighteningly graphic way) or by a lavish and elaborate ritual of atonement: Raskolnikov of *Crime and Punishment* and Mitya of *The Brothers Karamazov* are probably the most convincing examples of the latter.

It is inevitable that Dostoevsky, because of the Emperor's cruel joke, should devote so much time to last things; it is also understandable that he should seem so personally involved with both Godhood and the Christ figure. He wants, desperately, to believe in the palliating doctrine of Christ's uniting within Himself the dual roles of the divine and the human; and of course he believes in God. But the Prince reveals his author's misgivings. Above all, he raises ultimate questions: it will be, he says, a desperate gamble if we must depend upon Christ's humanity, because humanity is itself vain and riddled by imperfections. Man exerts himself to deserve damnation. Hence the Prince is surrounded by the most desperate characters, who either are afraid of their salvation (Myshkin is uncomfortably "too good" for them) or actively invite the ultimate punishment. The real difficulty in *The Idiot* comes from Dostoevsky's having almost from the beginning committed himself to Myshkin's failure. It is a strange tragedy that we behold. It may be, as Romano Guardini suggests, that the Prince fails because he is only a part of "a perfect 'impossibility,' "[13] though I think also that Dostoevsky is testing that fragment of the whole. Much is lacking here. There is almost no evidence of a transcendent goodness; rather, Myshkin's innocence is compared with the innocence of the child, with the unerring simplicity of the "blessed one," the idiot. R. P. Blackmur comes close to defining the problem when he suggests that the idiot is "the lay or private substitute for God who is blighted in the attempt to do God's work."[14]

There is, of course, the much honored idea of purity and innocence in the figure of the child. Myshkin had been told, as he himself admits, by his doctor in Switzerland that ". . . I was a complete child myself, a real child, in fact, it was only in face and figure that I was like a grown-up person, but in development, in soul and character and, perhaps, also in intelligence I was not grown-up, and I would stay like that even if I lived to be sixty." (*Idiot,* p. 101) The strategy is plain enough: Myshkin in his innocence will attract the most devious and conniving persons to confide in him; his childlike demeanor will provide a way to the confession of human evil. But there is a contrasting imbalance. As Myshkin is simply good, he will be susceptible to the worst views of his fellows. Not being "grown-up" exposes him to the most tragic insight into human nature. Dostoevsky seems to have put much trust in these images of innocence. They are always a way of reaching blessedness, but they present great hazards to the believing soul and the inquiring mind.

Ultimately the meaning of *The Idiot* comes down to the Holbein painting. Christ has just been brought down from the Cross; he shows obvious signs of physical damage, and mortality seems to dominate over the promises of resurrection and ascension. Dostoevsky seems to come to this conclusion against his will. He would much rather celebrate immortality and Christ's divinity, but he is overwhelmed by the evil in men, by their unwillingness to be saved, and he therefore poses Myshkin against his opposite, Rogozhin, one of the more darkly evil characters in all literature. Rogozhin is not just weak and liable to sinning; he courts evil, betrays it, exposes himself to it. "You dwell in darkness," Myshkin tells him when he first visits him. (*Idiot,* p. 238) Rogozhin considers himself from the start the Prince's antagonist, the evil to pose against his good. His mission is to prove Myshkin's innocence unavailing and ultimately of little use. Thinking later of his visit to him, the Prince reflects that

> Rogozhin was not just a passionate soul; he was a fighter for all that: he wanted to regain his lost faith by force. He had a tormenting need of it now. . . . Yes, to believe in *something!* To believe in *someone!*
>
> (*Idiot,* p. 263)

4

In the end, the antagonism is to lead to murder. After Nastasya is killed, as Rogozhin and Myshkin converse near her dead body, there is a commonalty in their moral natures. Both are finally reduced to an uncommunicative horror; both try to contemplate ways and means of forestalling a death that has already happened. They descend to the same level of helplessness in the face of death. Even though the one is an innocent observer and the other is a criminal, they are both implicated. Myshkin's "positive good" has failed to prevent the exercise of positive evil. We are left with the haunting image of Dostoevsky in the museum in Basel, staring in intense anguish at Holbein's depiction of Christ's mortality.

One of the important facts about Dostoevsky's novel is his having arranged the Christ figure to accommodate his argument. This is a common practice in modern literature. The Incarnation is more than an opportunity; it is a challenge, to use Christ as a means of analyzing the moral condition of man. In *The History of Jesus Christ,* Father R. L. Bruckberger has described the "central theme" of the Gospels as follows: "The conflict between time and eternity is the conflict appropriate to tragedy. It dictates the plot, which we call destiny. It is essentially a poetic conflict proper to every creation, including that of God." Certain heretics, he says further, "denied the reality of Christ's nature, maintaining that his body was only a paradoxical and tangible appearance, which veiled a nature at once glorious and impassive." Generally, moderns are inclined "to deny the invisible and to recognize in Jesus Christ only a man like any other."[15]

Father Bruckberger is probably correct; the tendency to "deny the invisible" does exist. But I should think also that the "visible" encourages writers to fashion the drama of the conflict to their own ends. This practice occurs, sometimes at least, as a consequence of doubt and fear similar to those shown by Dostoevsky. The Christian drama, the Passion of Christ, is indispensable to sanity and spiritual confidence. But there are many paradoxes and contradictions. Despite Father Bruckberger's dismissal as "mediocre Christians" of those whose fault is "not to hope enough,"[16] the drama of the Christ has taken many forms in modern literature, and it has been used for many objectives. The fascination (sometimes a happy confidence, sometimes a dread) of the story lies in the union of the universal and the particular, of eternity and time.

In his extensive *Systematic Theology,* Paul Tillich engages in an attempt to set boundaries to the matter. The two polarities, as Tillich sees them, are "the eternal truth" and "the temporal situation in which the eternal truth must be received."[17] This kind of theological definition requires what Tillich calls "situational religion," without which we have a "kerygmatic theology," one in which "the 'situation' cannot be entered; no answer to the questions implied in it can be given, at least not terms which are

felt to be an answer." (I, pp. 6–7) The basic theological claim of Christianity is that "the Logos became flesh, that the principle of the divine self-reve-
lation has become manifest in the event 'Jesus as the
Christ.' " (I, p. 16) Tillich insists that we can reach
transcendence by way of the "situational" and that
the experience of approaching it in this way is far
more rewarding than any other. Defining the phrase,
"The Son of God," Tillich says that it becomes "The
title of the one in whom the essential unity of God
and man has appeared under the conditions of existence. The essentially universal becomes existentially
unique." (II, p. 110)

The existential view of the Incarnation provides a
variety of perspectives, many of them attractive to
modern writers who are in their own way fascinated
by possible modern illuminations of the drama of
Christ. In some instances, as in D. H. Lawrence's
The Man Who Died,[18] the Christ story becomes the
beginning of a polemic, developing the author's own
special prerogative of interpretation. The most sin-
cere literary uses of the Christ figure have involved
the paradoxical vision of a divine being analyzed in
terms of His human uses and limitations. Nikos
Kazantzakis, perhaps the most vigorous of all who
have wrestled with the human issue in recent times,
may almost be said to have been obsessed with it and
its associated problems. The recently published *Report to Greco*[19] casts much light upon the role of the
Christ in his career. Like Dostoevsky, Kazantzakis
regarded the Christian myth and the existence of

God as indispensable to human sanity; both saw nothing but chaos without them:

> . . . Then I too began to discern the eternal, immutable face of God behind all religious symbols. And still later, when my mind grew overbroad and my heart overbold, I began to discern something behind God's face as well— chaos, a terrifying, uninhabited darkness.
>
> (*Greco,* p. 150)

The important fact, which echoes through many of his works, is God's challenge to man. God needs man; man must transcend his humanity, must through his spiritual vigor break through to God, who is calling out for his help.[20]

These are the strange premises of Kazantzakis' theology: that God cries out for our help; that we are all potentially "Saviors of God"; that our own journey upward is hedged and hampered by uncertainties, which we attempt to conquer by doubling and tripling our efforts, in an expression of emotional energy stronger than any other described in modern literature.

> Returning from Mount Athos, I felt for the first time that Christ wanders about hungry and homeless, that He is in danger, and that now it is His turn to be saved—by man.
>
> (*Greco.* p. 236)

The logic of this argument is simple enough. Like Miguel de Unamuno, Kazantzakis affirms the Passion story as indispensable to man. On a sea journey to Palestine, he saw the simple peasants who were his companions as they reacted to someone's telling them the story: "God, in their simple hearts, was once more taking on flesh, being crucified, saving mankind." (*Greco,* p. 244) The strong man, like his friend Zorba, will struggle to see that theology on this simple plane may endure and be preserved. But it is obvious to him that, while he may be searching for God, God is also searching for him.

> Every man is half God, half man; he is both spirit and flesh. That is why the mystery of Christ is not simply a mystery for a particular creed; it is universal. The struggle between God and man breaks out in everyone, together with the longing for reconciliation.
>
> (*Greco,* p. 290)[21]

This background will help us understand the curious nature of *The Greek Passion*[22] and *The Last Temptation of Christ*.[23] I should like to use the latter as an illustrative text. Several ideas seem pre-eminent in Kazantzakis' version of the Gospels: the struggle of man to become "godlike," which is the reverse of the coin; the paradox of the miraculous and the ordinary contained in one being; the paradox of the political implications of the Messiah; and, finally, the struggle between the Trinity and the One God (that is, the tendency to regard Jesus as on a level below the Trinity; this is perhaps an outgrowth of our doubts whether Jesus can actually be more divine than human, or whether, since He is human, He can be divine at all). The Christ of Kazantzakis' novel seems to be "tormented by God" to proceed to His mission;[24] the relationship he describes here appears to be similar to the Old Testament dialogues between God and the prophets.

Mary Magdalene plays an important role; she attempts to turn Christ away from his mission, toward becoming "normal," and she promises a life of this world, which he seems afraid to accept. (*Temptation,* p. 97) Judas in his own way urges him on, but to a messianic goal, a fight against the Romans, who are, after all, just men. Jesus has his own misgivings, which Kazantzakis very skillfully communicates to the reader. On the one side, God is "tormenting him" to complete his mission; on the other, the Jewish priest want "a sign," of his status and his function.

As a carpenter of Nazareth, Jesus has the task of making the cross on which the Zealot will be crucified. At this crucifixion, a startling and ominous event occurs:

> The gypsies, mounted on the rope ladders, had stretched the Zealot on the cross, keeping him tied with ropes so that he would not slip down. Now they took up their nails and began to nail his hands. Heavy drops of hot blood splashed Jesus' face. Abandoning his pickax, he stepped back in terror. . . . Trembling, he waited to hear the sound of ripping flesh. All his blood massed in the very center of each of his hands: the veins swelled and throbbed violently—they seemed about to burst.
>
> (*Temptation,* pp. 50–51)

This is most assuredly a "sign" to Him to be aware of His mission. It is also a terrifying experience, because it is dominated by the hot red blood, which tends to link Him with man, but will eventually also become a testimony of his being the "Son of God."

He continues to fight the mission, but it is a losing battle. For one thing, He does not seem to know what to say, a curious lacking in a moral leader of the people: "No, I'm no prophet; I'm just a plain, ordinary man who's scared of everything. . . ." (*Temptation,* p. 128) But God finally triumphs, as He was expected to:

> Jesus trembled secretly and struggled to find courage. This was the moment He had feared for so many years. It had come; God had conquered, had brought him by force where he wanted him—in front of men—in order to make him speak.
>
> (*Temptation,* p. 183)

This is the turning point; He denies his role of Jesus of Nazareth and becomes the son of His father, who is God. The idea of Jesus as Son of God is a difficult one for the Jews to accept; in their past history of the Old Testament, they have become accustomed to monotheism, to a God whose purpose was communicated to men by means of prophets. When Jesus enters the desert and is tempted by the Devil, we should now be ready to anticipate Kazantzakis' changes upon the Gospel version of Christ:

> . . . All nations have passed over her [Mary Magdalene], but it has been written in God's hand since your childhood that she is for you. Take her! God created man and woman to match, like the key and the lock. Open her.

Your children sit huddled together and numb inside her, waiting for you to blow away their numbness so that they may rise and come out to walk in the sun.

(Temptation, p. 257)

What follows in the progress of Jesus seems to be more a provincial rebellion (like that of the Cretans against the Turks) than it is the sacrifice of a God for all men. The Pharisees see in Christ a man who wishes to incite the people to rebel, "to divide our goods among the barefooted rabble." (p. 311) Jesus himself slowly becomes aware that He is to be the "Son of Man," not just a parochial leader. (p. 337) His sense of mission gradually turns inward, until He says to Judas, who is hot after the messianic sacrifice and the rebellion against the Romans:

If the soul within us does not change, Judas, the world outside us will never change. The enemy is within, the Romans are within, salvation starts from within!

(Temptation, p. 347)

The eight days of Jesus' agony and trial in Jerusalem begin with an artificial sense of triumph. He has provided "signs"; He has just raised Lazarus from the dead and so testified to His power. While He is Himself distressed over what He regards as the crudeness of the gesture, the people are impressed. It is only when He translates His mission from that of a parochial rebel to that of a universal spirit, a God doing God's will, that He encounters a mounting opposition. He is aware now that He must die, of His own will; He must be the "dying God." He wills that Judas betray him: ". . . it is necessary for me to be killed and for you to betray me. We two must save the world. Help me." (*Temptation,* p. 421) In the course of His two trials and of the ordeal before and after them, the Jews taunt Him for not having brought the kingdom of Heaven down to them.

The last temptation of Christ, in Kazantzakis' representation of the Passion, is a dream of ordinary happiness, corresponding to the temptation Satan had offered in the desert. "Everything was ready—the cross, the nails, the mob, Pilate—but suddenly an angel came and snatched you away." (p. 449) He is married to Mary Magdalene, to whom He confides that sex is the only route to immortality. But all of this, and more, is a part of His dream, and He awakens to the reality of the crucifixion just before He dies:

> He felt terrible pains in his hands, feet and heart. His sight cleared, he saw the crown of thorns, the blood, the cross. Two golden earrings and two rows of sharp, brilliantly white teeth flashed in the darkened sun. He heard a cool, mocking laugh, and rings and teeth vanished. Jesus remained hanging in the air, alone.
>
> (*Temptation,* p. 495)

6

In the course of the treatment of the Christ figure in modern literature, there are two principal kinds of emphasis: the "idea of Christ," or Christ as a type of hero who may be envied and even emulated; and the "historical Jesus," whose exemplary Passion may be used to illustrate a special modern disposition. Nathanael West's *Miss Lonelyhearts* (1933) is an example of the first; the hero moves from the cynicism of a modern newspaper columnist to an assumption of the Christ role. Kazantzakis' novel obviously belongs to the second group, but it has a special niche in our literary history. The humanity of Jesus dominates over His divinity for a long time, and then, in the end, takes over for a few minutes. The special role Kazantzakis sees for Christ accentuates his human, existential position, which grows slowly, first into an awareness of mission, then to an acceptance of it.

There are special, provincial reasons for his portrayal of Christ, just as paintings of the Christ figure have altered as time and place have dictated. But in his awareness of the crucial necessity of the Christian theology and in his willingness to come to its assistance, Kazantzakis offers a special interpretation of the role of Christ in relation both to man and God. One is here presented with the rather startling hypothesis that God needs us to help Him, so that He may save us.

NOTES

1. For a detailed discussion of these issues, see my *Samuel Beckett: The Language of Self* (Carbondale, Southern Illinois University Press, 1962), especially pp. 48–55 and ch. 5, pp. 138–53.

The Friends of God

2. See Plates 31 and 32 of Paul Ganz, *The Painting of Hans Holbein* (London, Phaidon Press, 1956).

3. Quoted by David Magarshack in his Introduction to *The Idiot* (Harmondsworth, Middlesex, Penguin Books, 1955), p. 7. All subsequent references to *The Idiot* will be to this edition and will be found in the text.

4. "Dostoevsky's Idiot, A Symbol of Christ," *Cross Currents* (1956), p. 378.

5. Cervantes' work is mentioned several times in *The Idiot*.

6. Letter to his niece, Sofia Ivanova, quoted in Ernest J. Simmons' *Dostoevsky: The Making of a Novelist* (London, John Lehmann, 1950): ". . . All writers, and not only ours, but even all Europeans, who have tried to portray the *positively* good man have always failed. Because this is an enormous problem. The good is an ideal, but this ideal, both ours and that of civilized Europe, is still far from having been worked out. . . ." (p. 166)

7. Quoted in Simmons, *Dostoevsky,* p. 164.

8. See Egbert Munzer, *Solovyev* (New York, Philosophical Library, 1956), pp. 11–27. "To actualize the potential Divine in man, is the aim of a Divine-human process, of an interaction between God and man. Only by this process in history can man restore his Divine likeness. . . ." (p. 27)

9. Letter of March 24, 1878, quoted in David Magarshack's biography, *Dostoevsky* (New York, Harcourt, Brace and World, 1963), p. 360.

10. The doctor who was in charge of the Swiss sanitarium from which the Prince had come.

11. See Edward Wasiolek, *Dostoevsky: The Major Fiction* (Cambridge, Massachusetts, the MIT Press, 1964): "The Prince is a failure as Christ was a failure, helpless to check the hurt that we do to each other, but ready to take it upon himself and by his own faith to give to all an image of the best of ourselves." (p. 109)

12. See Magarshack, *Dostoevsky,* pp. 122–24.

71

The Imagination's New Beginning

13. *Cross Currents,* p. 380.

14. *"The Idiot:* A Rage of Goodness," in *Eleven Essays in the European Novel* (New York, Harbinger, 1964), p. 144.

15. *The History of Jesus Christ* (New York, Viking Press, 1965), pp. 17, 22.

16. *Ibid.,* p. 55.

17. *Systematic Theology* (University of Chicago Press, 1951), Vol. II, p. 3. Other references to this edition will be found in the text.

18. *The Man Who Died* (originally published as *The Escaped Cock,* Black Sun Press, Paris, 1929).

19. *Report to Greco,* trans. Peter Bien (New York, Simon and Schuster, 1965). Greco is El Greco, a fellow Cretan artist, to whom Kazantzakis wishes to give the report of his struggles and adventures. Other references to this edition will be found in the text.

20. See *The Saviors of God: Spiritual Exercises,* trans. Kimon Friar (New York, Simon and Schuster, 1960): "My God struggles on without certainty. Will he conquer? Will he be conquered? Nothing in the Universe is certain. He flings himself into uncertainty; he gambles all his destiny at every moment." (p. 104)

21. In ch. 23 of *Greco,* Kazantzakis writes of having become acquainted with the works of Nietzsche: ". . . now I found myself too constricted both by contemporary man in the state to which he had reduced himself, and by Christ in the state to which He had been reduced by man." (p. 332).

22. Translated by Jonathan Griffin (New York, Simon and Schuster, 1959).

23. Translated by Peter Bien (New York, Simon and Schuster, 1960).

24. *The Last Temptation of Christ,* see especially pp. 30 and 183. Other references to this edition will be found in the text.

NOSTALGIA AND

CHRISTIAN INTERPRETATION:

HENRY ADAMS AND

WILLIAM FAULKNER

1

I WISH TO DESCRIBE A POINT OF VIEW AND ITS IM-
mediate historical background. The occasion was the
nineteenth century in the United States, when mate-
rial progress seemed to preclude meditation upon
meaning and destiny. We have any number of social
critics and intellectual historians to tell us just what
happened, and why it happened. Charles Walcutt
offers one version, an interesting one, and as plaus-
ible as most. In his *American Literary Naturalism,*
Walcutt speaks of the ambiguities of Emerson's influence on nineteenth-century American self-analy-
sis: "The essence of transcendentalism is to be found
in Emerson's repeated statement that Nature is a
symbol of Spirit. This means that what is ideal or
absolute is translated into physical laws and perfectly embodied (incarnated) as nature."[1]

Supreme idealism, an almost absolute confidence
in the mind's supervisory influence over physical nature, was bound to have a reverse effect, and Walcutt describes that effect, not only in the subtitle of
his book (*A Divided Stream*), but also throughout
his interpretations. "The transcendental ideal of freedom through knowledge [the mind knowing and controlling nature] expresses America's belief in science
and in physical progress as an image of spiritual
progress." (*Literary Naturalism,* p. 12) An almost
literal-minded assumption that the mind (which for
the most part was considered the "scientific mind")
controlled nature and acted upon it for its and our

good characterized the naïve, early phases of our commitment to science. Every conceptual principle somehow fell into line, justified science and was justified by it.

It was easy to align Protestant theology with the new scientific hypotheses concerning nature, man, and the universe. These developments had their own adverse effect; "Progress" was self-initiating and self-perpetuating; it needed almost no explanation, except in its results, and though religion was recognized and adjusted to, it lost its pervasive role. Emerson's religion was after all an extension of the substantial and initiating soul. But the application of spiritual confidence to the natural scene proved a not altogether happy event. Nature controlled by the transcendental soul was one thing, subordinated as it was to the most enthusiastic and the purest of egocentric philosophies. But somewhere along the line of its exploration of nature, the Emersonian mind was hit by the realism of its results; the *facts* of nature were not what the mind had insisted they should be. Mr. Walcutt describes this development as a kind of melodrama of nature's "hitting back." The facts that science discovered, and the inferences from these facts, tended to diminish the power of the mind; ensuing friction between mind and nature set up many of the "naturalistic" tragedies our literature of the late nineteenth century and early twentieth century gives us. The human self was indeed a diminished being, and ironically diminished because of its own initiative. Walcutt describes the conflicts in this way:

> There is always the tension between hope and despair, between rebellion and apathy, between defying nature and submitting to it, between celebrating man's impulses and trying to educate them, between embracing the universe and regarding its dark abysses with terror.
>
> (*Literary Naturalism*, p. 17)

In this context I am interested primarily in matters of cultural conflict. American embarrassment over superior European manners gave way to an acknowledgment that we were so busy exploiting nature that we could spare no time for the metaphors that might enable us to define ourselves. The energy that might have gone into adjusting theology to local circumstances was largely put into invention and progress. We were left, for the most part, with two major preoccupations, practical science and practical politics. The effect on our artists was surely predictable: on the one hand, there was the vast continent, where one made one's fortune in the manufacture of practical and therefore unmentionable objects; on the other, the journey to Europe to find, enjoy, observe, even purchase, its culture.

Theology was a major victim in this quick push into the twentieth century. R. P. Blackmur describes Henry Adams' "attractive force" as "the immediate relevance that his life and works have for our own,"[2] and it is true that Adams pointed out the risks our culture was assuming before most modern critics were able to appraise the consequences. No one was better suited or more lavishly endowed than he for surveying in depth and in breadth the nature of American culture: a descendant of two Presidents, private secretary to his father who was minister to Great Britain during the Civil War years and beyond, a Harvard student and later a professor of history at Harvard, a practising historian. All of these resources and gifts certainly put him in the best position possible for his long and probing analysis of American institutions and how they had fared in the crucial nineteenth century. Adams spent much of his time observing the political scene. He found it disappointingly shallow and expedient, but after writing two rather inadequate satirical novels about it, he decided to move beyond the particulars of Washington, D. C., to the more absorbing issues: our philosophical interests, the fate of theology in our culture, our special devices for accommodating ourselves to weaknesses in the cultural pattern we had not so much created as permitted by sufferance.

At the risk of oversimplification, I should like to push beyond Walcutt's descriptions and set up the terms of Americans' dissatisfaction. It was partly a matter of haste—to exploit the vast treasures of the continent, to establish a beachhead for the accumulation of fortunes. The real push came at the end of the Civil War; the years from 1870 to 1910 are filled with episodes of quick, even brutal, exploitation, as though there were no time to spare for anything but physical and financial maneuvers on the surface of

the land. But even in the midst of this hectic mal-
feasance, American intellectuals still managed to
puzzle over not only what our culture had but also
what it lacked.

For one thing, it lacked a past; the past was almost entirely in Europe. Tradition could not be
found, unless we moved Eastward and across the
Atlantic to seek it. The lack of tradition had another
effect. The distance from the time of religious secur-
ity and harmony was as long as the geographic distance was far. The consequent nostalgic pilgrimages
to Europe, to the very root sources of culture, affected our literature in no uncertain terms. The writings of Henry James and those of Mark Twain
formed the two poles of cultural attitude. Twain was
inclined to spoof the pilgrimages and to insist upon
a native, practical, and tangible world from which
a full measure of aesthetic and moral guidance could
he had. But James' characters were seldom satisfied
with staying in America; they needed somehow to
expose themselves to the great masterpieces of culture—Paris, Florence, Venice, Rome—in order to
be "completed" or "resolved" or "fulfilled." The
"passionate pilgrimage" was largely a matter either
of acquiring manners or of seeing how much one has
lost through his not having attended to a lively and
sensitive world. Lambert Strether of *The Ambassadors* (1903) is perhaps his most notorious instance.
In his case, and in others, James equates the intensity and beauty of a charming world with "living";
Strether has not "lived" in Woollett, Massachusetts,

and he warns his young friend, little Bilham, not to repeat his (Strether's) mistakes:

> . . . The affair—I mean the affair of life—couldn't, no doubt, have been different for me; for it's at the best a tin mould, either fluted and embossed, with ornamental excrescences, or else smooth and dreadfully plain, into which, a helpless jelly, one's consciousness is poured—so that one "takes" the form, as the great cook says, and is more or less compactly held by it: one lives in fine as one can. Still, one has the illusion of freedom; therefore don't be, like me, without the memory of that illusion. . . .[3]

His lost opportunity was, actually, the result of his choosing not to stay in Europe and Paris at an earlier time. But there is more to it than that. A graceful though sad irony plays upon Strether's latter-day discovery of what he has lost, and there is no real certainty that he can define his loss, beyond calling it "Life," a term he defines to himself as "life anywhere but in Woollett, Massachusetts." There is no assurance that James went much beyond setting up imaginative conventions according to which life could most suitably be lived. He rarely invoked metaphysical issues, and the international comedy of manners was chiefly worked out in terms of distinctly and specifically practical moral engagements. James had some idea of a refined European society, signified by elaborate and tastefully appointed country houses, that was being threatened both from within and from without. But he was not so superficial as to assume that Europe was ipso facto a symbol of the refined and the fulfilled life. He did not go much beyond the thesis that the human consciousness needed its proper setting and the stimulus of a gracious tradition in order to thrive and to grow.

2

Adams differed substantially from James: first in having a sense of political history; second in being interested in the major metaphors by which a culture might be defined and described. George Hochfield has described Adams' interests in this way:

> Adams began, like many another in the nineteenth century—Melville, for one—with an inner compulsion to find a substantial ground of moral value outside of himself: in society, in nature, in history. Without believing in God, he yet demanded that such value have an absolute sanction based on an ideal or transcendent reality.[4]

In so desiring to explain himself and his country by means of a moral or theological force outside himself, Adams was following the urgent suggestion of his own experience. The metaphors of politics available to him were superficial; social mannners had no such interest for him as James' had had for *him;* as for religion, he went back to the Puritans of the seventeenth century, and their successors in his own time gave no reassurance that religion explained what was happening to him and to his culture. *The Education of Henry Adams* is a revealing document in this connection. In it Adams is looked at from a narrative perspective; it is he, "Adams," and never "I," who is involved. Thus he was able to span the major periods of the nineteenth century as though he were writing a fiction about it. The book is primarily an analysis of forces that underlay the superficial politics and manners of his century. As such, the *Education* is what George Hochfield has called "the essential history of his time."[5] Like most artists, but more skillfully in attending to the specific needs of interpretation, Adams had recourse to major symbols which, at the risk of some oversimplification, tended to hit at the center of important issues that many contemporaries saw only vaguely.

To begin with, there was the idea of man as the sum of the forces that influenced him; that is, each period of history drew man toward a major center of energy. This center was the major symbol of its time. This was a doctrine of "Power," but there were conflicts, largely the result of the inadequacy of a theology to explain a power in its current form. The special metaphoric use of the word "Education" was to explain how he, Adams, was educated to *fail* in his attempt to understand the present, and the future toward which his culture was moving. He was anxious to find an inclusive explanatory metaphor, and failed many times in seeking it. He needed above all to transcend the minutiae of trivial, parochial explanation provided by the politics and journalism of his time, and even currently accepted scientific theories. His career as an historian of American politics had been undertaken primarily in the interests of discovering if, "by the severest process of stating, with the least possible comment, such facts as seemed sure, in such order as seemed rigorously consequent, he could fix for a familiar moment a necessary sequence of human movement."[6]

But Adams was out for a more ambitious view. Clusters of facts, however arranged with whatever integrity and care, could not explain why, and the explanations he had inherited were too limited to accommodate what was currently happening. He must somehow find a major symbol which would assimilate the vocabulary and the phenomena of current science.

> . . . Copernicus and Galileo had broken many professorial necks about 1600; Columbus had stood the world on its head towards 1500; but the nearest approach to the revolution of 1900 was that of 310, when Constantine set up the Cross. The rays that Langley discovered, as well as those which he fathered, were occult, supersensual, irrational; they were a revelation of mysterious energy like that of the Cross; they were what, in terms of medieval science, were called modes of the divine Substance.
>
> (*Education,* p. 383)

Adams began by fastening upon the idea of man as so much expendable energy, which could be attracted to a central symbol, whichever was dominant. He continued the fancy by suggesting that, contrary to his education, the energies of man shift their attractions and are influenced by new symbolic centers. Subsidiary definitions included a change in rituals: the World's Fair of 1900 had replaced the medieval Mass, etc. In short, Adams was to use theologies as a part of a larger scale of definition and explanation. The two major symbols of his argument were those of the Virgin and the Dynamo. As for the first, Adams devoted most of an earlier work, *Mont-Saint-Michel and Chartres* (1904), to it. It was scarcely appropriate to our present culture, partly because of the American attitude toward the Virgin and toward women generally:[7]

> . . . . The knife-edge along which he must crawl, like Sir Lancelot in the twelfth century, divided two kingdoms of force which had nothing in common but attraction. They were as different as a magnet is from gravitation, supposing one knew what a magnet was, or gravitation, or love. The force of the Virgin was still felt at Lourdes, and seemed to be as potent as X-rays; but in America neither Venus nor Virgin ever had value as force—at most as sentiment. No American had ever been truly afraid of either.
>
> (*Education*, p. 383)

3

Adams' history comes down to the playing of polarities against each other. The opposing attraction was the medieval world of the twelfth and the thirteenth centuries. In going back to the Middle Ages, Adams shared with his contemporaries a fairly common disposition toward the past, which was in effect an extension of the move backward and away from the nineteenth-century present. The word nostalgia at least partly explains it. But it was mainly a search for a missing culture, the location of which was for a majority in Europe and in time from the twelfth century through the sixteenth. The characters of Adams' fellow artists went to Europe for two reasons: in search of a gracious society, that was admittedly fighting a losing battle against "modernity" but still retained much of the charm and many of the monuments of the past; and in the interests of exploring a richer, non-Puritanic world and at least of testing its dominating theology. The monuments were, of course, mainly buildings—mostly churches, places of worship. These had the great distinguishing feature of concentrating on an object of attention, or at most a very few, as contrasted to the multiple function of the political buildings, with a different function for each windowed segment, or the skyscraper, whose pointing upward falsified its intention, which was to accommodate a thousand diverse, mundane, and horizontally arranged interests. Architecture was the principal aesthetic means of intellectual definition.

In the spirt of his search for this kind of meditation, Adams described his travels in 1895 from the Abbey of Mont-Saint-Michel through Normandy to Chartres. The book he wrote is in one sense (a superficial sense) a guidebook, and there have been many readers who accepted it as such. But beyond that service, the experience served as the basis for Adams' intellectual exploration of the European Middle Ages, the Cult of the Virgin, and the symbolism resulting from a way of life that centered upon a worship and ritual architecturally governed by the shape and the particulars of a cathedral.

Adams' special kind of nostalgia led him to meditate upon the directive energies which had led to the structure of these French places of worship. The medieval Catholic theology was at the center of his deliberations, but these were informal and aesthetic and could not at all have passed any formal examination in theological proprieties. His main concern was to find the exact center of "force" in the Middle Ages, and he believed that—in view of both its politics and economics—it could be read from the architecture of the time. The route from Mont-Saint-Michel to Chartres was in itself a challenge to his very active historical imagination. He had earlier found nothing but chaos in trying to put phases of intellectual history together,[8] and turned (from 1894–1900) to the symbology of force to secure a more elaborate scheme of interpretation. Ultimately three symbols occurred to him: the Cross, for the early centuries of the Middle Ages; the Virgin for the twelfth and thirteenth centuries; the Dynamo for the twentieth. Each of these was the center of a field of force which attracted energies to it. For his time at least, and on his terms, Adams had found an adequate means of educating himself.

The force of *Mont-Saint-Michel and Chartres* is primarily aesthetic and emotional, and in that respect particular and diversified; yet it acted to draw the energies of man (through his building the cathedral and worshipping within it) toward it as a center. There was a conflict between the theological abstraction and the imperfect human particular, but it was both resolved and preserved by the figure of the Virgin, who was both related to and independent of the Trinity. In this way unity allowed for diversity and multiplicity without destroying itself. Adams raises some strange and interesting questions concerning this pattern:

> . . . No one has ventured to explain why the Virgin wielded exclusive power over poor and rich, sinners and saints, alike. Why were all the Protestant churches cold failures without her help? Why could not the Holy Ghost —the spirit of Love and Grace—equally answer their prayers? Why was the Son powerless?[9]

These are more than merely empty questions. The answers Adams provided are various, sometimes quite unusual, but all of them reflect the late nineteenth-century Protestant American looking nostalgically at an early culture and theology and trying through them to take hold of his own. Adams speaks with some subtlety and skill of the human attitude toward absolutes, since it is absolutes that puzzle him: they are necessary for any true grasp of reality, but they are also frighteningly pure and demanding.

> . . . The Trinity feared absorption in her, but was compelled to accept, and even to invite her aid, because the Trinity was a court of strict law, and, as in the old customary law, no process of equality could be introduced by direct appeal to a higher power.
>
> (*Chartres*, p. 289)

"She was imposed unanimously by all classes," Adams continues, "because what man wanted most in the Middle Ages was not merely law or equity, but also and particularly favour."

The main reason for her strength was that man was a sinning creature and needed an intercessor, as Dante had discovered, before he could tolerate or be tolerated by an Absolute. And Adams insists that the Trinity is an Absolute; he all but forgets and ignores the Incarnation. In any case, he says, the Christ represented at Chartres (despite His having held up hands, to display the stigmata) was an earlier Christ, and depended upon the Mother for sustenance and greater meaning. The men and women responsible for building—and at least on one occasion rebuilding—Chartres Cathedral knew themselves to be sinners:

> . . . They were all criminals; if not, they would have had no use for the Church and very little for the state; but they had at least the merit of their faults; they knew what they were, and, like children, they yearned for protection, pardon, and love. This was what the Trinity, though omnipotent, could not give. . . . [God] could not be human and imperfect, nor could the Son or the Holy Ghost be other than the Father. . . .
>
> (*Chartres*, p. 290)

It was important to accept God, from whom all realities came; but the issue was itself not entirely clear, and had to be accepted on faith; and in any case, man needed a person whom he might approach as a supplicant. This is the truth Adams reads in the

Cathedral; the architecture is itself awe-inspiring, but the sculpture and the stained-glass break it down into the particulars necessary to sustain one's explicit acceptance, above and beneath his faith. In an interesting sense, the architecture of Chartres as a whole presents the universal and the sculpture and stained glass the texture, the particulars; these latter are absorbed by the pattern of the whole.

> . . . Mary concentrated in herself the whole rebellion of man against fate; the whole protest against divine law; the whole contempt for human law as its outcome; the whole unutterable fury of human nature beating itself against the walls of its prison-house, and suddenly seized by a hope that in the Virgin man had found a door of escape. . . .
>
> (*Chartres*, p. 307)

In one place Adams identifies this rebellious gesture with the general sense of irritation over Puritanism in Europe and America.

> Mary's treatment of respectable and law-abiding people who had no favours to ask, and were reasonably confident of getting to heaven by the regular judgment, without expense, rankled so deeply that three hundred years later the Puritan reformers were not satisfied with abolishing her, but sought to abolish the woman altogether as the cause of evil in heaven and on earth. The puritans abandoned the New Testament and the Virgin in order to go back to the beginning, and renew the quarrel with Eve.
>
> (*Chartres*, p. 308)

This is no frivolous remark. Adams is too much

aware of his own time and his own culture, in which the role of women is much too limited, leaving the masculine drive toward power almost without check. He does not look forward to the achievement of ultimate power, which he anticipates but suspects he is too old to live to see. In his analysis of the religious art of this French cathedral, he has left no doubt of his preference: that power in itself must be palliated by a force indifferent to it, yet not inclined ultimately to oppose it; that the great theological abstraction in medieval history was the Trinity, which was nevertheless controlled by the spirit of the Virgin; that Puritan influences downgraded Mary, if they did not remove her altogether; that, in consequence, the move toward power all but proceeded without hindrance.

4

Adams is not satisfied with a formal explanation of the difference between the Middle Ages and his own times. The look backward is nostalgic, and there is no question that the Dynamo will replace the Virgin as symbolic center at great cost and probably with tragic results. Both Adams and James posed the feminine consciousness against the more austere and less comprehending masculine one; and both were aware that the deliberate reduction of the feminine role had helped to diminish woman's true cultural function, which was to appeal to man's awareness of himself as imperfect, human, and liable. The loss for American culture was hard to measure, though it is discussed in a number of works by Adams' fellow artists; Edith Wharton's *The House of Mirth* (1905), *The Custom of the Country* (1913), and *The Age of Innocence* (1920) are conspicuously based on the sad premise that the general cheapening of a woman's place in society led to a general reduction of moral probity in the conduct of daily affairs. The fear of this consequence is more implicit than explicit in most twentieth-century literature. Willa Cather frequently—as in *O, Pioneers!* (1913) and *My Ántonia* (1918)—portrayed the feminine strength and power of endurance in a frontier society, but her heroines did not prevail against an onrushing move toward total mastery of nature. *The Professor's House* (1925) shows the feminine influence all but vanished.

In the literature of post-World War I, the tone has changed. Hemingway had his own kind of respect for women, but then they were his own kind of women.[11] The work of James T. Farrell and John Dos Passos is so often dominated by their kind of ideological maneuver that neither men nor women come through clearly. Nathanael West has a deep sense of fear and hurt concerning the modern scene, but his major savior is almost exclusively the impulse of a Christ in an indifferent modern society. In *Miss Lonelyhearts,* the Christ imagery refers almost exclusively to the suffering Christ, who is taking on the ills of an entire society without any truly clear

91

sense of why He is doing so: the shadow of a lamp-post "pierced him like a spear" (p. 23); the gray sky "held no angels, flaming crosses, olive bearing doves, wheels within wheels" (p. 25); the idea of Christ had often excited him when he was a boy, "But the moment the snake started to uncoil in his brain, he became frightened and closed his eyes." (pp. 39–40)[12] When Miss Lonelyhearts goes to his death, it is as much to quiet his own uneasiness and to rid himself of the agony of watching the unhappiness and absurdity of the human race. West is too much taken up by the immediate fears and the future perils of his society to give the Christ image any real theological position or function.

The fullest American treatment of the Passion of Christ in recent years is in Faulkner's *A Fable*. There are several complex implications here. For one thing, the book is not consistently a "fable," nor can it be considered an allegory; although there are many suggestive parallels, not once is the New Testament actually mentioned or the characters labeled to suggest a direct relationship to the story of Christ. The setting is World War I, during the fighting of which Faulkner was a young man, so that perhaps he felt closer to it:[13] For reasons any experienced Faulkner reader will immediately recognize, he did not choose the American Civil War for his setting, despite the superficial idea that it would seem to have been much more suitable. *A Fable* is by no means a novel, despite the thread of narrative that does manage to come through the rhetoric; it is, instead, a post-

Stockholm parade of Faulkner's humanist orna-
ments, headed by the affirmations that man will not
only endure, that he will prevail.

A Fable is also a culmination of years of speculation over the Christ image in Faulkner's career.
Just what these earlier allusions to Christ mean, it is
difficult to say. Benjy Compson is thirty-three years
old on Easter Saturday, 1928; Joe Christmas's ini-
tials are of course J. C., and the length of his passion
matches that of Christ's. The list can be added to,
and a recent critic has said that these allusions are
not just coincidental; they *must* mean something![4]
What they mean is perhaps best explained by Faulkner himself, in one of his conversations with University of Virginia students; answering a question
about "the basic crucifixion image" in his work, he
said:

> Remember, the writer must write out of his background.
> He must write out of what he knows and the Christian
> legend is part of any Christian's background, especially
> the background of a country boy, a Southern country
> boy. My life was passed, my childhood, in a very small
> Mississippi town, and that was part of my background. I
> grew up with that. I assimilated that, took that in without
> even knowing it. It's just there. It has nothing to do with
> how much of it I might believe or disbelieve—it's just
> there.[15]

It is obvious that, whatever his disposition to what
is "just there" in his background, Faulkner wrote *A
Fable* in a certain access of nostalgia over what the
Christian story must some time ago have meant, as

compared with what it means now. The discussion of Southern Protestant (white) parishes contrasts glaringly with his much more vivid recital of the Reverend Shegog's sermon in Part Four of *The Sound and the Fury* (1929). Faulkner wished somehow to make as much out of the Passion story as possible, without literally committing himself to its meaning. As a result of this wish, and of accompanying rhetorical excesses, the impression is rarely vivid and the narrative line is so slender as to end by convincing few and confusing many. Irving Howe says of *A Fable* that "it lacks the charm and human suppleness of the Gospel according to Matthew, the text on which it partly depends. . . ."[16] He goes on to call the book an example of "the yearning so common to American writers for a 'big book,' a *summa* of vision and experience, a final spilling-out of the wisdom of the heart." (pp. 268–69)

Perhaps one of the most interesting criticisms comes from Ernest Sandeen, who admits that Faulkner clearly intended the Corporal to be a Christ figure; the parallels are too obvious to deny the ultimate analogy. But these parallels are used at Faulkner's discretion. Like Lawrence, West, and other modern writers, Faulkner has taken fragments of the Passion when it suited him to do so. The references to Christ and to the Passion, says Professor Sandeen, "are in the nature of allusions, of extended figures."[17] The basic source of Faulkner's confusion is that the novel is not Christian, but Manichaean.[18]

Citing a late passage from *A Fable,* Sandeen says that it

> . . . perversely attributes a gnostic or manichaean outlook to Christ and at the same time an incarnational outlook to the Church. Christ has here been separated from its Founder because the supernatural has not been taken into account. The Corporal in Faulkner's novel has not been created in the image of Christ; instead, Christ, represented here [p. 364] as a "furious and intractable dreamer," has been recreated in the image of the corporal. The critical fact of the Incarnation, the very fact which has given the Church its scandalous faith in the human as well as its transcendent faith in the superhuman has been left out of consideration. (pp. 65–66)

A Fable is, like Adams' *Mont-Saint-Michel and Chartres,* a nostalgic view of a religious past which seems menaced by present conditions. Like Adams' work, it is an essay in definition, in which the terms are forces, and the parallel of present with past made to suit the circumstances. Hence the theological uses made in each are fragmentary and distorted. Nevertheless, there was no special reason that Faulkner needed to be theologically accurate; he needed only to prove the significance of the particular use to which he wanted to put the Christ story. That use is clearly humanistic; there are no evidences of the supernatural, no real attempt to associate the Christ image with the Trinity. What remains is an analysis of human behavior and a suggestion of its exemplary nature.

Regardless of what the doctrinal beginnings

seemed to have been, the value of *A Fable* must come from its success in revealing man in crisis, or man reacting to crisis, or man transcending his limits. When we look at it in this way, we discover that its importance depends upon a slender line of affirmation: man will endure, man will prevail. These are the assertions he made at Stockholm in December, 1950.[19] They are primarily the result of two emotions: nostalgia over some "impossible time" when man *could* endure and prevail; fear that he may never again do so. The challenge to the hero's humanity is always accompanied by grave doubts of his ability to rise to it: in Kazantzakis' *The Last Temptation of Christ* (1960), George Bernanos' *The Diary of a Country Priest* (1936),[20] West's *Miss Lonelyhearts.*

A Fable fails, not only because its hero does not meet the terms of his action, but also because these terms are not clearly shown. For as Sandeen maintains, there is no real anguish, either in a Gethsemane or on a Calvary; indeed, the Corporal is almost flippantly scornful of all of the proceedings. Further, much of the action is almost improbably coincidental. So that the parallel of Christ and the Unknown Soldier, which might have given the book a strange power,[21] is too casually accidental to be effective. As Olga Vickery has pointed out, the action is *intended* for at least three levels of revolt: through the implied analogies with the New Testament, the Corporal rebels against *institutional* Christianity and prefers to challenge it in his archetypal

96

personality; but he is never really developed as a Christ, so we must accept his rebellion as purely personal, with an exemplary suggestiveness or "message"; finally, his rebellion is in some mysterious way linked to the search for natural freedom conducted by the Groom and his two Negro companions on the junket through the American South.[22]

It is not easy to point to Faulkner's real intentions in *A Fable*, but there are some aspects of it that can be discussed. For one, he assumes an ideal human condition, which has been violated wilfully and selfishly. This condition involves, for one thing, the privileges of human privacy,[23] which of course are violated with a brutal thoroughness in a wartime setting. The crowd that watches the burning of Joanna Burden's house in *Light in August* (1932) here stands in intensified bewilderment and moral paralysis, desperately in need of some example and clue of individual action:

> . . . the whole Place one aspic of gaped faces from which rose that sound not yelling but half murmuring and half wailing. . . .[24]

In Faulkner's highly involved rhetoric, the masses here become linked to history and to a form of "evolutionary primeval slime," a strangely contradictory reference to the disciplinary effect of the military upon them, "eyeless and tongueless on the floor of the first dividing of the sea, palpant and vociferant with no motion nor sound of its own but instead to some gigantic uproar of the tides' mighty copula-

tion. . . ." (*A Fable,* p. 225) It is obvious that this
"protoplasm" is designed to be brought under con-
trol as the result either of military authority or of
free will. But to influence even their free will requires some discipline, and the Corporal's behavior
is almost entirely free and obstinately rebellious. In
fact, Faulkner suggests two choices of human reaction, human rapacity (suggested by the marshal)
and free choice. Rapacity endures, the old general
says, "not even because it is rapacity but because
man is man, enduring and immortal [in the sense
that he will "prevail"]; enduring not because he is
immortal but immortal because he endures. . . ."
(*A Fable,* p. 260)

Apparently the Corporal and the old general
arrive at the same conclusion via distinctly different
routes:

> . . . I don't fear man [says the general]. I do better: I
> respect and admire him. And pride: I am ten times
> prouder of that immortality which he does possess than
> ever he of that heavenly one of his delusion. Because
> man and his folly—"Will endure," the corporal said.
> "They will do more," the old general said. "They will
> prevail."
>
> (*A Fable,* p. 354)

Although the general recognizes the power of man
to survive anything that may try to subdue him, he
must put down the present mutiny, in terms of immediate circumstances. Either the Corporal must be
won over, or he must be dispensed with, for the
"greater" good. The Corporal acts out the role

Faulkner has given him: a creature of extreme free will, who must never be unsure of his actions, must never be dissuaded from his objective. The priest who has been asked to attend him before his death warns him of the sin of pride:

> . . . Beware whom you mock by reading your own mortal's pride into Him who died two thousand years ago in the affirmation that man shall never never never, need never never never, hold suzerainty over another's life and death. . . .
>
> (*A Fable*, p. 363)

The Corporal behaves in the tradition of Faulkner's best Yoknapatawpha specimens. He is free even of that freedom with which the old general tempts him; and he is free apparently of any clear motive for being free, beyond the fact of his intensely, obsessively persisting in his freedom. This is the point to which the virtuous Faulkner hero moves. It is not a place in history, though if one had to date it generally, it would have to be in the past. The Corporal dies, not for a cause, not in answer to an appeal, or pressure, or a demand, from a higher being, or from any human being.

Unlike Henry Adams', Faulkner's sense of history is almost entirely parochial; since his understanding of the New Testament is by acknowledgment that of "a very small Mississippi town," his use of it will be special and narrowly provincial, except where it is wildly imaginative. It cannot be historically or doctrinally explained. It is the result of his having viewed both the present condition of his world and the past reasons for it, and then tried to set up the terms according to which human action can somehow bring this condition back to an "Edenic" level. But he has also needed a framework for such a narrative, so he chooses that of the Gospels—chooses, but not entirely, not all the way, only to suit his ends and purposes. As a result, the action of *A Fable* is strangely truncated and only capriciously meaningful. It is surely a strange fable! And in his curious handling of the terms of parallelism, Faulkner seems almost typically "modern."

NOTES

1. *American Literary Naturalism: A Divided Stream* (Minneapolis, University of Minnesota Press, 1956), p. 10. Other references to this edition will be found in the text.

2. "The Expense of Greatness," in *The Expense of Greatness* (New York, Arrow Editions, 1940), p. 253.

3. *The Ambassadors* (New York, Scribner's, 1909), I, 218; originally published 1903.

4. George Hochfield, *Henry Adams: An Introduction and Interpretation* (New York, Barnes and Noble, 1962), p. 130.

5. *Ibid.*, p. 116.

6. *The Education of Henry Adams* (Boston, Houghton Mifflin, 1918), p. 382. Other references to this edition will be found in the text.

7. Henry James and Henry Adams were conspicuous exceptions to this attitude toward the role of women in culture and society. James put women in the center of a drawing-

room convention, while Adams gave her a symbolic, an apostatized, meaning.

8. See Hochfield, *Henry Adams,* p. 102.

9. *Mont-Saint-Michel and Chartres* (Garden City, New York, 1959), p. 288. Other references to this edition will be found in the text. Originally published 1904.

10. See James Hastings, *et al.,* ed., *A Dictionary of Christ and the Gospels* (Edinburgh, T. and T. Clark n. d.), I, pp. 686–89.

11. See Robert W. Lewis, *Hemingway on Love* (Austin, University of Texas Press, 1965).

12. *Miss Lonelyhearts* (New York, Liveright, 1933). See Victor Comerchero, *Nathanael West: The Ironic Prophet* (Syracuse University Press, 1964.)

13. He did not fight in it but did get in a little training with the Royal Canadian Air Force, in Canada.

14. See John W. Hunt, *William Faulkner: Art in Theological Tension* (Syracuse University Press, 1965), p. 20 and *passim.* "The Christ symbols refer beyond themselves; they are used as a part of a total fictional strategy. They may, of course, be poorly used, but in any case they never stand alone as the carrier of the novel's import." (p. 20)

15. In *Faulkner in the University,* ed. F. L. Gwynn and J. L. Blotner (Charlottesville, University of Virginia Press, 1959), pp. 85–86. Cf. pp. 17, 21, 27, 62, 68, 117. In his last statement on the subject in this book, Faulkner says, à propos of *Light in August,* that "that Christ story is one of the best stories that man has invented, assuming that he did invent that story, and of course it will recur. Everyone that has had the story of Christ and the Passion as a part of his background will in time draw from that. There was no deliberate intent to repeat it [in *Light in August*]. That the people to me come first. The symbolism comes second." (p. 117)

16. *William Faulkner,* 2nd ed. (New York, Vintage,

1962), p. 269. Other references to this edition will be found in the text.

17. "William Faulkner: His Legend and His Fable," *The Review of Politics,* 18 (January, 1956), 50. Other references are in the text.

18. See Father William Lynch, "Theology and the Imagination," *Thought,* 29 (Spring, 1954), 67–68, in which he discusses the fascination modern writers have for manichaean images.

19. See *Faulkner: Three Decades of Criticism* (East Lansing, Michigan State University Press, 1960), pp. 347–48. For a very favorable analysis of *A Fable,* see Heinrich Straumann's "An American Interpretation of Existence: Faulkner's *A Fable,*" trans. Grace A. Goodman and Olga W. Vickery, in *Three Decades of Criticism,* pp. 349–72. This essay originally appeared in German, in *Anglia,* 1955, pp. 484–515.

20. Translated by Pamela Morris (New York, Macmillan, 1962). The parallel of the priest with Christ is not insisted upon, and in any case the priest distinguishes himself by suffering passively a symbolic "cancer" and not failing its demands.

21. The Christ as soldier-victim has been presented occasionally with some power. See Fritz Unruh, *Way of Sacrifice,* trans. C. A. Macartney (New York, Alfred Knopf, 1928).

22. See *A Fable,* pp. 151–204.

23. See the essay, "On Privacy," in *Essays, Speeches, and Public Letters,* ed. J. B. Meriwether (New York, Random House, 1965), pp. 62–75; originally published in *Harper's,* July, 1955. Here Faulkner expresses great irritation over our not having learned the lessons of true privacy, in which we might truly contemplate "things of the human spirit." (p. 75)

24. *A Fable* (New York, Random House, 1954), p. 137. Other references to this, the first edition, will be found in the text.

INDEX

von Abele, Rudolph, 46n
Adam, Karl, 16n
Adams, Henry, x, 77–91,
95, 99, 100n
The Age of Innocence
(Wharton), 91
The Ambassadors (James),
79–81
Aquinas, Thomas, 27, 34
Aristotle, 40–41

Baudelaire, Charles, 7, 18n
Beckett, Samuel, vii, 2–3,
17n, 35, 50, 70n
Bernanos, Georges, 96
Blackmur, R.P., 37, 59, 77
The Brothers Karamazov
(Dostoevsky), 54, 58
Bruckberger, R.L., 61–62
Bultmann, Rudolph, 34

Cather, Willa, 91
Chartres Cathedral, x, 87–
90
Christ
    passion and death of, ix,
    14, 64–65, 67–69, 92–
    100
    two treatments of, in
    modern literature, 69–
    70
Christianity, and modern
science, 11, 83–84

Clemens, Samuel, 79
"The Comedian as the Let-
ter C" (Stevens), 35–36
Conrad, Joseph, 56–57
Creation, artistic, and reli-
gion, 4–5, 49–51
Crime and Punishment
(Dostoevsky), 58
The Custom of the Country
(Wharton), 91

Dante Alighieri, 88
De Quincey, Thomas, 7–8
Descartes, René, 2
*The Diary of a Country
Priest,* (Bernanos), 96
The Disappearance of God
(Miller), 7–8, 18n
Dos Passos, John, 91
Dostoevsky, Fyodor, 49,
51–60
Dubliners (Joyce), 31, 32,
38
Duncan, Edward, 46

*The Education of Henry
Adams* (Adams), 81–84
Eliot, T.S., 8
Ellmann, Richard, 19n, 29–
30, 45n
Emerson, R.W., 9–10, 75
Esthétique du Mal (Ste-
vens), vii

Index

A Fable (Faulkner), 92–102

Farrell, James T., 91

Faulkner, William, 92–102

Faulkner in the University, 101

Finnegans Wake (Joyce), 21, 28, 30, 34, 43, 45

Fitzgerald, F. Scott, 57

Flaubert, Gustave, 8

Four Quartets (Eliot), 8

Friedman, Maurice, 16n

Glicksberg, Charles I., 16n

Goldberg, S.L., 42–43

Grass, Günter, 6, 18n

The Greek Passion (Kazantzakis), 65

Guardini, Romano, 51–52

Hamlet (Shakespeare), 41

Hartt, Julian N., 16n

Heller, Erich, 17n

Hemingway, Ernest, 91

Hochfield, George, 81–82

Holbein, Hans, 51, 57, 60, 61

The House of Mirth (Wharton), 91

Hunt, John W., 93, 101n

Ideology, and theology, 4

The Idiot (Dostoevsky), 51–61

Imagism, 31–32

Incarnation, 5, 8–9, 10, 14, 52, 54, 62–63, 88

James, Henry, 79, 80–81, 90, 100n

Joyce, James, ix, 2–3, 5–6, 20–47

Joyce, Stanislaus, 32

Kazantzakis, Nikos, 49, 63–69, 70, 96

Kenner, Hugh, 46–47n

Killinger, John, 16n

The Last Temptation of Christ (Kazantzakis), 65–69, 72n, 96

Lawrence, D. H., 63, 72n

Light in August (Faulkner), 97, 101n

The Little Review, 45n

Litz, Walton, 31–32, 45n

Lubac, Henri de, 17n

Lynch, Father William, 102n

Magarshack, David, 71n

Malraux, André, 9

The Man Who Died (Lawrence), 63, 72n

Miller, J. Hillis, 3, 7–8, 10, 17n, 18n

Miss Lonelyhearts (West), 70, 91–92, 96

Mont-Saint-Michel and Chartres (Adams), 84–90, 95

Mueller, Lisel, 6–7

My Ántonia (Cather), 91

Nobel Prize for Literature (Faulkner), 96

Index

Notebooks (Dostoevsky), 53

O, Pioneers! (Cather), 91

Poets of Reality (Miller), 3–4, 10, 17n
A Portrait of the Artist as a Young Man (Joyce), 21, 22–33, 36–40, 43–44
Poulet, Henri, 18n
Pound, Ezra, 15, 33–34, 46n
The Professor's House (Cather), 91
Puritanism, 76–77, 85, 87, 89–90

Report to Greco (Kazantzakis), 63, 64, 65, 72n
Riddel, Joseph N., 19n
Robinson, E.A., 9

Sandeen, Ernest, 94–95
The Saviors of God: Spiritual Exercises (Kazantzakis), 72n
Shakespeare, William, 41
Simmons, Ernest J., 71n
Smidt, Kristan, 38–39, 46n
Solovyev, Vladimir, 53–54, 71n
The Sound and the Fury (Faulkner), 94
Stephen Hero (Joyce), 21, 22, 31, 32, 38
Stevens, Wallace, vii, viii, ix, xiii, 9, 11, 15–16, 17–18n, 19n, 35–36
Straumann, Heinrich, 102
Sultan, Stanley, 47n

Systematic Theology (Tillich), 62–63, 72n
Szczesny, Gerhard, 17n

Tanner, Tony, 9–10
Theology, and ideology, 4
Thrane, James R., 45n
Tillich, Paul, 62–63
Twain, Mark (*see* Clemens, Samuel)

Ulysses (Joyce), 5–6, 18n, 21, 22, 28, 30, 31, 32–33, 38, 39–42, 43

Unamuno, Miguel de, 64
Unruh, Fritz, 102n

Vahanian, Gabriel, 16n
Vickery, Olga, 96–97, 101–102n
Vico, Giambattista, 34
Virgin Mary, as symbol, 85–86, 87, 89, 90
A Vision (Yeats), 14

Waiting for Godot (Beckett), 50
Walcutt, Charles, 75, 76–77, 78, 100n
Wasiolek, Edward, 71n
The Way of Sacrifice (Unruh), 102n
West, Nathanael, 70, 91–92, 96
Wharton, Edith, 91

Yeats, W.B., ix, 9, 11–14, 27

Zorba the Greek (Kazantzakis), 65

FRANCO HARRIS

PHOTO CREDITS
All photos by Carl Skalak, Jr.

Published by Creative Educational Society, Inc.,
123 South Broad Street, Mankato, Minnesota 56001
Copyright© 1977 by Creative Educational Society, Inc. International
copyrights reserved in all countries.
No part of this book may be reproduced in any form without written
permission from the publisher. Printed in the United States.
Library of Congress Cataloging in Publication Data
Braun, Thomas, 1944-.
Football's powerful runner, Franco Harris.
(All-star series)
SUMMARY: A portrait of an outstanding running back who holds the record
for yardage gained during a rookie season.
1. Harris, Franco, 1950-   —Juvenile literature.
2. Football players—United States—Biography—Juvenile literature.
[1. Harris, Franco, 1950-   2. Football players] I. Title.
GV939.H33B7   796.33'2'0924 [B] [92]   76-44440   ISBN 0-87191-585-5

FOOTBALL'S
POWERFUL RUNNER
FRANCO HARRIS
BY THOMAS BRAUN

CREATIVE EDUCATION/CHILDRENS PRESS

4

Number 32 just stood there in the end zone holding the ball. For a moment no one in Pittsburgh's Three Rivers Stadium could believe what had happened.

A few seconds earlier, the Steeler quarterback, Terry Bradshaw, had thrown a last desperate pass. The crowd groaned as the ball bounced away from the intended receiver.

Huntting 5-1-78 6.60-4.95

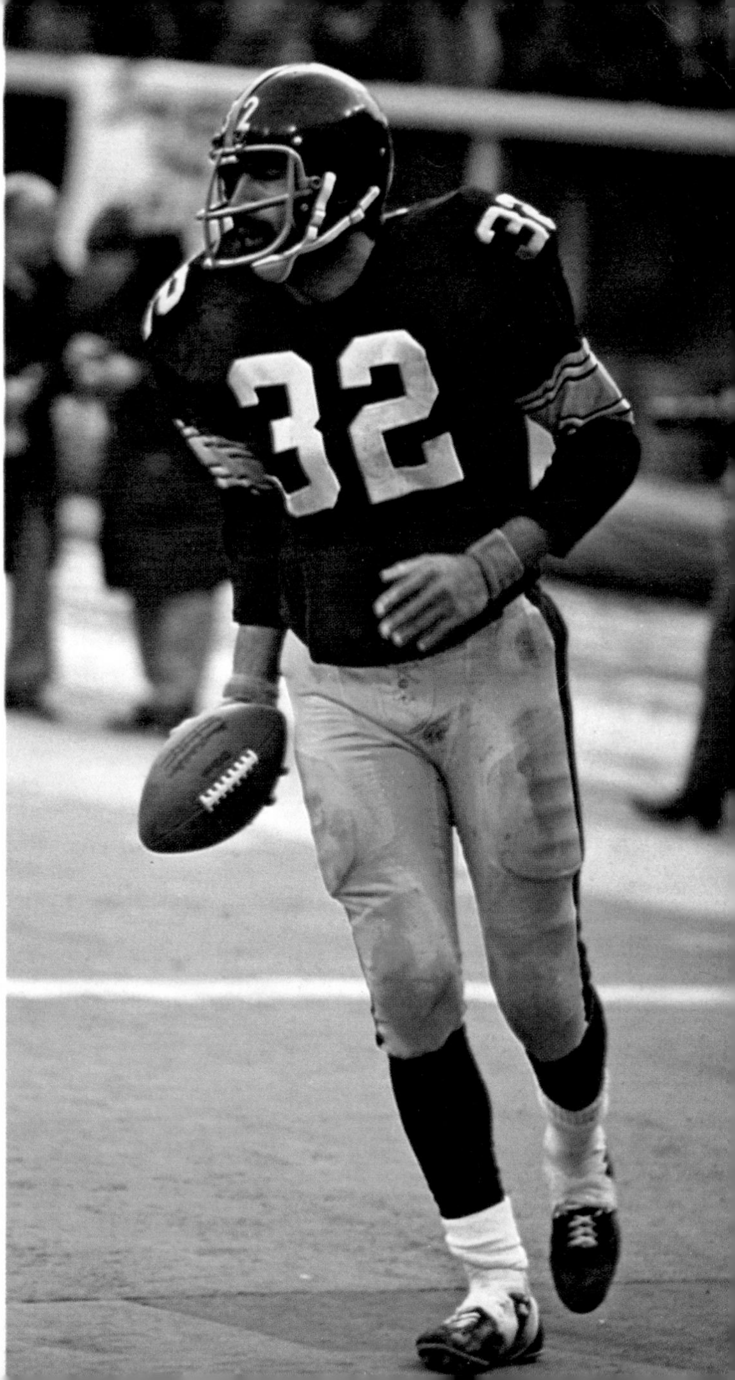

6

The football should have hit the ground. The game should have ended. The Oakland Raiders should have defeated the Pittsburgh Steelers in this 1972 AFC play-off game.

But while the deflected pass was still in the air, Franco Harris reached out and grabbed it. He pulled the ball to his chest and exploded 42 yards to score Pittsburgh's winning touchdown.

8

Franco's impossible catch and his team's last-second victory made it clear to everyone that something new was happening in Pittsburgh. After 40 years without a championship of any kind, the Steelers had finished the regular season in first place.

They had a new coach and a strong, young team. But the main reason for their first winning season was Franco Harris, the best rookie running back in the league.

10

Franco developed his skill as a powerful runner when he was young. His family lived near the Fort Dix Army Base in New Jersey. At the base Franco worked at many different jobs.

When he wasn't working he was running. Franco loved to run. At night he and his friends held footraces on the street in front of their apartment.

12

Franco played his first game of organized football in junior high school. Later, at Rancocas Valley High School, he became an instant star.

In his first high school game he carried the ball for an 84-yard touchdown. During his junior year, he led his team through an undefeated season scoring 20 touchdowns. In that same year he was named a high school All-American.

Franco's brilliant high school career caught the attention of many college football scouts. He visited nine different schools and decided to attend Penn State.

14

With the Nittany Lions of Penn State, Franco ran for 2002 yards in three seasons. He also carried the ball across the goal line 24 times.

While Franco was scoring touchdowns for Penn State, the Pittsburgh Steelers were building a new football team.

Chuck Noll became the Steeler coach in 1969. He took over a team that had won only four games in the previous two seasons. In his first year Noll's team lost all but one of 14 games. Five wins in 1970 were followed by six in 1971.

The 1972 college player draft was held in February. Coach Noll knew that his team needed a strong running back. Noll had seen Franco run and liked his size and speed. In the first round of the draft, the Steelers picked Harris.

Franco was happy to be selected in the first round. But at the same time he was disappointed. He knew that the Steelers had one of the coldest records in the NFL. He wanted to play for a team that was hot.

18

At the first team meeting, the rookie from Penn State heard his new coach greet the players with optimism. The Steelers were steadily building toward a winning team. Noll looked forward to the new season with confidence.

Franco listened to the coach's words and tried hard to believe them.

Noll was right. Pittsburgh won all but one of its exhibition games.

20

Franco carried the ball ten times in the first regular season game. He discovered quickly that regular season play was different from the kind of football played during the exhibition season.

When the games really counted, the pros got serious. They moved quicker and hit harder. Holes in the defensive line disappeared too fast for Franco to sneak through them.

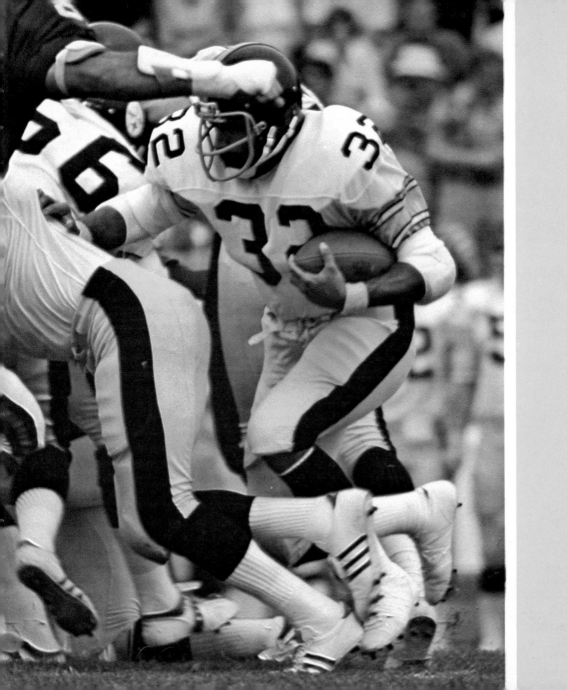

22

In the fourth game of the season Franco was determined to do what he did best. He ran straight and hard. He didn't wait for holes to open. He made his own holes instead.

The new straight-ahead strategy worked. By the final gun Franco had scored one touchdown and had carried the ball a total of 115 yards.

Both Franco and the Steelers were developing a real taste for winning.

24

Nothing could stop Franco from running. Like an Amtrack Express he rushed through Buffalo, Cincinnati, Kansas City, Cleveland and Minnesota.

By December he had gained over 100 yards in each of five straight games. The record for a rookie was six.

With five minutes left in the next game, Franco's rushing total was only 65 yards. Before the game ended he carried six more times and finished with a 102-yard total.

He had tied the record set in 1957 by another brilliant rookie, Cleveland's Jimmy Brown.

26

The Steelers didn't make it to the Super Bowl in 1972. But at the end of that season, no other team in the NFL had a more promising future.

The American Football Conference Rookie of the Year title went to Franco Harris. He had galloped 1055 yards in his first year as a pro. In the history of football, only four other players had gained more than 1,000 yards in their rookie seasons.

28

It took the Steelers two more years to work their way to their first Super Bowl. In January, 1975, they met the Minnesota Vikings in New Orleans and came up with an easy win.

In this single game, Franco carried for 158 yards — two yards more than the entire Viking team had run in all three of its Super Bowl losses.

The next year the Steelers returned to the Super Bowl and beat the Dallas Cowboys.

30

The best way to judge a team is to check the record book. One of the best judges of a running back is another running back.

Jimmy Brown once said, "If I was starting a team tomorrow, and had first choice of any runner in pro football to build my backfield around, I'd pick Franco Harris."

BILLIE JEAN KING
O. J. SIMPSON
EVEL KNIEVEL
HANK AARON
JOE NAMATH
OLGA KORBUT
FRAN TARKENTON
MUHAMMAD ALI
CHRIS EVERT
FRANCO HARRIS
BOBBY ORR
KAREEM ABDUL JABBAR
JACK NICKLAUS
JOHNNY BENCH
JIMMY CONNERS
A. J. FOYT

THE ALLSTARS